Goddess and the Madness

By

Michi Nadler

Acknowledgements

I would like express my gratitude to God almighty, the Universal power, always within us and around us, as we awaken to our true nature and free ourselves from suffering.

I would also like to thank all the saints, teachers and spiritual friends who helped me along the way to see the light.

I would like to thank Nirmala and Nancy White who helped me write and edit the stories and Gary Every for his advice and encouragement in creating this book.

Finally, I would like thank my husband, Gary Nadler, who has supported my journey with unconditional love, and his editing efforts.

Cover photo by Gary Every

Dedication

I dedicate this book to all seekers of Truth.

Table of Content

Unusual Beginning

"Suffering is part of our training program for becoming wise."
-Ram Dass

Where does anyone begin to tell the story of his or her life's transformation, especially when the story includes so many discouragements, obstacles, challenges and sorrows? Yet, at the same time, the same story may include great beauty, valuable lessons, amazing experiences and limitless love. This is my story: one of a survivor who overcame life's obstacles and created her own dreams. It is the proverbial story of the ugly duckling that discovered she was really a regal swan.

Born into a broken family, I was the youngest daughter of five children. Although there are no pictures of me as an infant, my brother told me I was an ugly baby. He compared me to a little monkey, with far too much hair and homely features. Also, I was born with many serious health challenges. As a young child, I was exposed to radiation, most likely from the numerous military conflicts experienced by the divided Koreas and the two atomic bombs dropped on Japan just nine years before. I simply had very little vitality to function properly and enjoy my life, from childhood and into most of my adulthood. I recall that whenever I attempted to play, I would fall to the ground from exhaustion, continually scraping my knees. I was clumsy and uncoordinated, so consequently I spent most of my days lying down and reading books. Almost any activity required more energy than I had. Even tying my shoes led to twisting my ankles and falling. To this day, I have problems with my ankles and knees, perhaps from falling all the time as a child.

I spent many days by myself or in the company of my beloved mother. My siblings were all much older than I, so I didn't have them for company. Only my mother was there for me. One of my earliest and most vivid memories of her was feeling her tears wetting my face and hair as she held me close to her breast. As a youngster, I did not know the reason for her acute sorrow, but I found out later.

As a maiden, my mother married a successful doctor. He was a gynecologist and together they had several children. He was a good father and husband and a caring doctor. In fact, he died from a brain hemorrhage on the way to save a mother and her baby. After his death, my mother met my biological father, and I was the result of their brief love affair. They did not marry and the resultant pregnancy caused me and my mother much heartache. The townspeople ostracized her and even before I was born, her in-laws took her to court for all the marital assets she was left as a widow.

Months went by and life got so bad for my mother that she wanted to kill herself. In Korea at that time, having an illegitimate child was probably one of the worst things that could happen. In the Korean culture, there was no forgiveness for the shame that accompanied this situation. I believe if it weren't for her love and devotion to me, my mother would have ended her life. I was her baby girl and we were connected in a very special way, sharing the shame of my birth and the love that grew out of that pain.

After her in-laws made life unbearable with threats and ultimatums, my mother finally gathered the courage and means to move to another town. She fled the cruelness of Inje with me and my siblings and moved to Chunchon, the capital of Gangwon Province, South Korea. As a single woman with five children, my mother had to work very hard to make ends meet. She acquired a big house with six rooms and rented out rooms to students and professionals, all while caring for her children and taking in odd jobs. We did not have luxuries, but we had basic food and clothing plus the strong sense that our mother loved us very much.

Growing up, I did not feel any acceptance in this new town. When I registered for school in Chunchon, everyone noticed I had a different last name from my siblings, and so the cruelty and ostracization began and I was shunned again. Throughout my childhood, I have vivid memories of walking into a room that was loud and boisterous with conversation, only to have it turn deadly silent or, even worse, hear the whispers behind my back. I knew I was the subject of their low voices and hushed tones, but I did not understand why.

Perhaps my interest and devotion to God was a result of this difficult childhood. I remember that my devotion to God began as a toddler. As young as four, my fervor and reverence for God was unusual and extraordinary. I once saw a statue of Jesus atop a church, complete with thorns and blood, and I was instantly overcome with love and adoration. I declared Jesus to be my husband! This was such an intense experience, especially for a young child, and it was the most powerful emotion I can remember. It took the place of everything else, giving me hope and a sense of purpose.

I also loved reading the Bible. I am sure I did not understand what it was saying, although when

I read passages such as, "If you know the truth, the truth will set you free," it resonated in my heart like beautiful music and I could sense this amazing wisdom. Similarly, I could appreciate the wisdom in the story of the adulterous woman, when everyone wanted to stone her for her societal sins, Jesus lovingly said to the judgmental crowd, "He among you who has not sinned, cast the first stone." These pearls of wisdom rang true to me, even as a young child and I recall sleeping with the many Bibles I had collected. When most children had stuffed animals as their bedtime companions, the numerous bibles I had collected in various languages became my night-time friends and comfort.

I also recall, as a young adult, taking it upon myself to "save" my fellow townspeople. I would walk down the street and brazenly ask, "Would you like to be saved?" If they said yes, I would relate to them the four Principles of Christianity, which I learned from Campus Crusade for Christ – 1) Adam and Eve ate the apple against God's instruction; 2) Since then, all of us are separated from God; 3) God sent his only begotten son, and, lastly; 4) The son is the way, the truth, and life. If we believe in Him, we will be saved. If the townspeople accepted these principles, I would ask them to pray with me and then boldly declare,

"You are saved." This is how I remember speaking to the townspeople.

I remember when the evangelist, Billy Graham, came to Korea and I became active in his ministry. I repeated the Four Principles, as stated above and taught by Minister Graham, and then created the group, "High School Campus Crusade for Christ (HCCC)." I am sure I didn't understand it fully, but it was appealing and interesting to me on so many levels. I wanted to know "the truth," and I wanted to know what "salvation" meant. However, at that time, I did not have the understanding I have now, knowing that "salvation" means "liberation."

Although being "saved" by a young child may seem outrageous in the western world, in Korea, religion, whether Christianity or Buddhism, was very much an integral part of the culture. I feel Koreans are captivated by religion and spiritual practices, more so than in Western cultures. Churches and temples dot the cities, villages and countryside. I began attending Sunday school and church on my own, although my brothers, always controlling, tried to force me to stop attending. They were Buddhist and did not appreciate my yearning for Christ.

Even though my brothers made attending church difficult, it was not their harassment that eventually ended my relationship with the Christian church in our town. The church itself caused my disillusionment. As I grew into a teen, I began to notice that, for the most part, the church leaders seemed to argue often over money and politics. This caused me much heartbreak because I felt they were not expressing the qualities of Jesus or his teachings. I had no real reason for loving Jesus as I did, but I did. When I did not "find" Him in church, I became brokenhearted and disillusioned.

Once, I had contemplated becoming an evangelist, or maybe even a preacher in a church. Then, I wondered, "What good would that do? Can I actually meet Jesus that way?" All the activities I was involved in, since I was four years old, did not fulfill my spiritual needs, so I basically stopped attending church. I never went back and no one ever questioned where that devout young lover of Jesus went. The church members never seemed to care.

I spent most of my teenage years, lost in books, looking for answers to a life that had little hope. I did not know what I was searching for, but I knew, deep down, there had to be something more. Life couldn't just be the misery I had experienced on a day-to-day basis. I was sickly, had no friends and was ostracized from every social function. No wonder I was a lonely and depressed child.

Once, in response to my utter despair, I literally stopped speaking for two years. I wanted nothing to do with my surroundings or the people in it. It drove my mother and my teachers crazy, when they would ask me a question and I would not answer. I was simply shut down from a world I considered heartless, inconsistent, and erroneous, without any obvious rhyme or reason. I was deeply depressed with thoughts like, "This mortal life, here on Earth, cannot be the end of it. It is so imperfect; there has to be something better than what I am seeing around." I learned about the greatness of Jesus, Buddha, and other saints, but I did not see them anywhere. Perhaps they didn't exist. Where were they? Longing to find illuminated beings was the theme of my life from an early age.

As an avid reader, when I found the book, *Siddhartha*, I was immediately captivated. Here was a handsome prince, willing to sacrifice everything, just to know himself. As Siddhartha grew from a child to an adult, his intelligence was matched with a compassionate gentleness. Unlike his peers, he spent most of his time alone, wandering the palace gardens. Like me, he did not participate in the common games of children but sought the company of books and nature.

In his deep desire to become a monk, this well-to-do Prince stood diligently day and night, waiting for his father, the king, to give him permission to become a man of God. I immediately recognized his fortitude and determination. I saw myself in Siddhartha, who was determined to find God or Truth, and become enlightened, even if I didn't really know what it meant at that time. All I knew was I had a deep inner yearning that transcended materiality and rested in spirituality.

Inspired by Siddhartha, and on summer vacation from high school, I went to a Buddhist temple and asked them to take me as a novice nun. I was accepted and we had a ceremony, complete with shaving my head and dressing me in traditional robes. They gave me a "mother" mentor, who became very attached to me. Against the rules, she brought me candy bars and included me in the nun's conversations about sex and how to eat meat and eggs without getting caught by the higher echelons of the Temple. They would laugh at how there was a special way to order food in restaurants so that the meat would be hidden under the noodles, thus keeping their supposed "sin" from the public. I soon felt that there was nothing spiritual about these nuns, and like the Christians in my town, I thought these nuns led a double life. They claimed to be religious and spiritual, but they did not take their vows seriously.

In response, I went to a small temple looking for the sincere spirituality I had read and dreamed about. Unfortunately, the smaller temple was worse. It was like a little secular family, complete with all the day-to-day idiosyncrasies. The teacher I yearned for did not reside in this temple either. I quickly learned the error of my choice and left that temple, as well.

Similar to the Christian church where I did not find Jesus, I did not find Buddha in the Buddhist temples either, since the monks and nuns were surprisingly non-Buddha like. Perhaps I did not recognize what spirituality was or I didn't know what to look for. Maybe Buddha was represented there, but I failed to recognize Him.

These thoughts churned in my head and I became more depressed, lost and unappreciated by the world. I had little to offer, since I was in poor health with little or no finances, no father, and a suffering mother. I thought to myself, "Why should Buddha or Jesus come to me? I have nothing to offer God." So I sunk lower into the rock bottom of my depression and planned to return home.

On my way, I stopped by my brother's house. I had no hair, since I had shaved it all off while at the Temple and I was thin, weak and run-down. When my younger niece saw me in the house, she didn't recognize me because I was wearing a hat. Cautiously, she approached and took off my hat. Seeing me bald, she began to scream. Her screams brought my brother, who was a policeman, running. As an officer, he assumed that any girl without hair must have been to jail. In response to his wrong assumption, he began to beat me. Crying and begging him to stop, I tried to explain where I had been. Once he realized his mistake, he felt terrible and tried to make it up to me by taking me to a movie. After all, to him, I had followed a noble calling and pursuit.

Healing

"Know the truth, and the truth shall set you free."
-John 8:32

Struggling with my health was my life's history. I knew with agonizing familiarity what poor health was like, each breath an energy-draining chore.

Not only did I suffer from physical issues, connected to exposure from radiation, but I had to deal with the deep-seated emotional issues I had absorbed from the time of my conception. In Korea, the cultural shame of the illegitimate nature of my existence has always been with me, unconsciously, until I recently became aware of them.

As a child, I remember watching other children play and if I tried to join in, I would most often find myself crumpled on the floor. I was exhausted beyond description. I thought an inclined position was normal and the other children were the odd ones.

However, I survived and grew to be an adult. I seem to have had an amazing ability to conjure up every bit of energy to be functional, since I had to be successful in business. At that time, I was both a real estate agent and later a stockbroker!

Could I have found more stressful jobs? I would wake up at 4:00 a.m. and go to work twelve-hour days in the hustle and bustle of Los Angeles, really functioning like a zombie. I would stop at the office on my way to show a property and appear like the walking dead to the other agents. But, as soon as I needed to meet with a prospective client, I gathered every ounce of inner strength and did my job well.

This went on for several years until one day in 1985 when I was supposed to get up and start my usual hectic day; I felt as if I had awakened from a dream, where I had floated off into what I perceived was heaven or paradise.

In this place, I floated, not walked, toward a beautiful marble palace, where beautiful flowers were everywhere, all perfectly shaped and radiating bright vivid colors. Even the mountains surrounding this place felt celestial. As I floated through this wonder, I encountered a being who was sitting on a lotus dressed in traditional Korean clothes. I then realized that this person was my very own mother. My heart opened as I looked upon her face and I wanted to run to her, but then I realized I couldn't move or speak. Telepathically, I said to her, "Mother, life is so hard on Earth. I don't want to go back. I want to stay here with you." My mother just closed her eyes and waved her hand as if to say, "Go away."

Confused, I tried again. "No, please, don't make me leave. I don't want to go back. I don't want to experience any more pain. Please."

But she did not relent. Instead, she lovingly took my hand and led me, floating, outside. She explained to me, also telepathically, "This is not your time. You have much more to do."

When she released my hand, I woke up from this altered trance-like state. As I opened my eyes, I realized that it was late morning and the sun was relatively high in the sky. I thought to myself, "It is Monday. I must get up, as I have meetings and a ton else to do. I am late." Expecting everything to be normal, I attempted to get out of bed, but couldn't move a muscle. "Was I dead?"

I told myself, "Move your arms or your legs," but no part of me obeyed. I couldn't distinguish my own heartbeat, not even the slightest palpitation. "I must have been dead, visited my mother in paradise and now I am still kind of dead." I thought all this without any emotion and just waited for something to happen.

It was over two hours before I could begin to move my fingers, one at a time. This experience was so devastating physically, that it adversely affected my kidneys, with a condition that took me over a decade to heal. This traumatic experience put even more stress on my already weakened body.

Physically, I was a mess for most of my life. I never had a normal menstrual cycle. I always had bad eyesight and wasn't blessed with very good teeth. Internally, I have dealt with a sluggish digestive system and constipation. I had "mysterious" skin conditions throughout my life, and constant fatigue was normal. As I awoke that Monday morning, I had never been in such terrible shape, so weak and pitiful. I even prayed for death, anything to end this pain, weakness and hopelessness. I thought to myself, as I lay in pain and depression, "I won't live long enough to meet Jesus or Buddha. I will never find an enlightened teacher, or meet true saints." I can still remember the tears and emotion I felt, trying to restore my energy, so I could sit rather than being horizontal all the time.

In 1990, after semi-recovering from my complete exhaustion in Los Angeles, I was somehow able to move to Sedona. I was still weak and in poor health, when fate intervened once again. As I was walking along Oak Creek one day, I slipped on a wet rock, fell about 5 feet, landed on my left hip and broke the bone. I could not move without pain for about a month. Suddenly, while lying on my right side, I started to feel feather-like sensations throughout my body, which then became very intoxicating, almost like being drunk. I noticed that these feelings, floating around and within my body, were very healing, diminishing my pain and cultivating much bliss. So falling and breaking my hip led me to a life-changing and Kundalini awakening experience. That shock to the base of my spine was a cosmic incident that woke up the "mysterious serpent power."

This experience changed my life dramatically, revealing all the spiritual possibilities that I knew should and could exist. This energy surge actually gave me the ability to function while I was healing my emotional and physical blockages. It guided me and took care of me in all the other details of my life. I thought, "Someone must be looking out for me and taking care of me and maybe God is finally knocking on my door. Perhaps God will be paying my bills, helping me sleep and cooking my food." This whole experience eventually led me to meet Papaji, and my other teachers, and then brought me to my present day life. After my Kundalini awakening, I acknowledged, for the first time, I could be healed and may even find God in the process.

Those earlier years, after the Kundalini opening, were not a very comfortable or easy time.

There was so much purification happening that while this energy penetrated different areas of my body, I would make involuntary mudra-like movements, like in dancing and bending. Sometimes, I would find myself in some yoga posture I saw in books that I never imagined I could ever do, like bending backwards and making a complete circle with my body. At times, I would make animal-like expressions and movements and at other times I would assume a meditation posture and go into a blissful state. I was having visions of "the other world," saw a dragon, thousands of Buddhas and Jesus. Inside, I was amazed beyond imagination, feeling as though my prayers had finally been answered. From this time on, my life took a dramatic turn toward a wonderful spiritual journey which I had thought could only exist in dreams. My life became enriched with enlightened spiritual teachers, friends, monks and swamis, some of whose stories appear later in this book.

For about 10 years, I could not function normally in the world, which was inconvenient to say the least. Many of the spiritual phenomena I experienced appeared to be purification processes and there were several months when I sat motionless without food or speech. One of my friends would give me a straw to sip water and then help me to the bathroom. For me, these years revealed another realm or reality not of this physical world. Remarkably, this energy even took care of the many details in my life, while I was sitting motionless, dissolving the illusions of this dimension. At this time, I was guided to visit India, seeing certain pilgrimage sites and meeting with Papaji and other teachers, swamis and saints. But mostly, I drifted in a motionless Samadhi state, while this energy helped me get from one place to another. I knew I was being taken care of and I just followed the magic. This energy seemed to dissolve my individual self and reveal a much larger SELF. It brought stillness to my heart, which slowly allowed me to love the world and its people, not always an agreeable proposition. This energy was my true teacher, guiding me to other teachers and experiences and protecting and empowering the whole process. I understood that this energy is dormant in everyone and just needs to be awakened. I realized that this energy is also called the "Holy Spirit," "Shakti," "Kundalini," and "Serpent Power." It also has the ability to undo the illusion that has been created. All these phenomena I experienced, which put me out of commission, were to help my purification, reawaken my soul and bring the essence of silence, peace, and love to me. And in time, as the purification of my mental tendencies continued, my powerful "monkey-mind" began to lose its grip. Life became more fun and much easier to handle. This energy simply dissolved the duality and I transformed into Oneness, All-knowingness and enhanced intuition, where wisdom and truth were revealed. There were no more tears of hopelessness, or longing for the truth and trying to survive. There was an effortless abundance of bliss and happiness on all levels.

When I came back to Sedona from my second trip to India in December of 1999, even though I had more energy to function, my body was still very broken. An acupuncturist told me that my kidneys were malfunctioning, but pure Shakti (energy) was holding me up. There seemed to be two different lives going on within me; one, my challenged physical body and the other, a newly born spiritual body.

In the summer of 2001, I met my future husband and chiropractor, Gary. In 2005, we built and opened our Wellness Center. This is where I learned various healing modalities, began working on my physical health and helped others with theirs. One by one, the healing modalities were presented to me and I was guided on a physical healing journey.

I learned Ayurveda in India and in Albuquerque at the Ayurvedic Institute with Dr. Ladd. I went to New York to study Bio-Resonance and Biological Medicine and learn how to use the Lecher Antenna. I went to Seminars and workshops on behalf of my husband and learned Chinese Medicine, mineral balancing and Vibrational Medicine. In our Wellness Center, I incorporated all this new information along with an Infra-Red Sauna and colon hydro-therapy. Somehow, I was shown where to focus my attention.

Little by little, I began to feel better physically than I had before. I began to bury all my Spiritual Journey experiences in a file and went to work in our Wellness Center creating a business and learning more about healing the physical body. I became rather successful with a large clientele, but in my office, no one really knew what had previously happened to me. Of course, after ten years of meditation, marriage and dealing with the world, this was yet another level of purification. I spent much time in introspection, witnessing resistance and the tendency for ungodly qualities inside. The spiritual knowingness and beauty I had experienced was kept secret from the world, while I played the game of being a therapist, staying in my comfort zone most of the time. In 2007, I began to have severe symptoms inside my throat where large blood bubbles would form and periodically pop, sending sprays of blood out from my mouth. As hard as it is to believe, I ignored this as much as I could. Years went by and the condition came and went, but was never resolved. I used the knowledge I had gained thus far to address this problem, but it would come and go, surface and resurface.

In the spring of 2014, seven years after first becoming aware of my throat condition, I knew it was time to face this condition head on. I realized that I had been afraid to speak about my spiritual experiences and what I had learned all these years. Even though I had opened the Wellness Center, no one, not even my husband, knew about my spiritual background. I knew there was a unique and strong connection between health and spiritual energy, but I chose not to share that part of myself. I did have a sense that someday I could add the spiritual part into my healing services, even though I had put a lid on all the stories and events I had experienced before.

I saw that this severe throat condition, which seemed to come out of nowhere, signified I could no longer be silent. I needed to speak out, talk and write. I felt, deep in my heart, that I could not be silent about what I knew, so I had to share my experiences. I understood that if I didn't speak out and share, I would surely be dead from throat cancer, or some similar affliction, within a few short years.

Previously, whenever my teachers, psychics and astrologers told me that I would be a spiritual messenger, I really didn't feel comfortable with the thought of my being a "spiritual figure" in public. Perhaps I was not ready or it wasn't my time. Since I was mostly introspective and introverted, I just wanted to be left alone in that cave. But this throat condition made me see that it wasn't my choice. The healing was in releasing the resistance to write, speak and share what I knew. It didn't seem to matter if my words reached one person or one hundred thousand. I just needed to fulfill my dharma, share what I knew, tell my experiences and be released from my physical prison.

The individuals who walk through the Wellness Center's doors are there for a reason, never by accident, but through a higher force. In a wellness business sense, I was busy and successful. But I knew that the true healing for people would be spiritual, and yet, I had resistance expressing that part of myself.

Some of my clients, who are also healers, told me repeatedly that I was ignoring my dharma and often said, "If you don't teach, you will soon die from some serious condition or have a car accident."

Therefore, it became obvious to me that I needed to take the lid off my innermost part and share it with others. This is how this small book came about. Since I started writing, my throat condition improved dramatically and I began to feel more comfortable talking about spiritual matters.

"If you want to find the secrets of the universe, think in terms of energy, frequency and vibration."
-Nikola Tesla

Goddess of Love

"Where there is love, there is life."
-Mahatma Gandhi

Guanyin is commonly defined as an East Asian spiritual figure associated with compassion and mercy. She is considered a Bodhisattva, a person who is able to reach nirvana but delays doing so out of compassion to save suffering beings. The name Guanyin is short for Guanshiyin, which means, "Perceiving the Sounds (or Cries) of the World." In my heart, I feel that Guanyin is the universal image of the Goddess of Love and Compassion. To me, she represents the Great Mother, or the Divine Mother. Guanyin is an icon of unconditional love, one of many beautiful feminine qualities of God. In all spiritual paths, there always seems to be a female image that represents the feminine aspect of the universe. Mother Mary, White Tara, Guadalupe and Guanyin have all been represented throughout the ages as the Goddess or Divine Mother. In my perception, Guanyin conjures up images of the feminine personality of God, yet there is no gender attached to universal, unconditional love or creation. In the bigger picture, "unconditional love" is androgynous.

I have been told many times over the years by seers, psychics and saints that I was the embodiment of Guanyin. Most of the time, this seemed to be quite ridiculous to me, but after my intense Kundalini awakening experiences, my sense of Guanyin started to unfold with both inner and outer experiences. The affinity that I have had with Guanyin throughout my life seemed unclear before my Kundalini experience. But afterwards, a sense of clarity emerged that helped me put into words what I had been feeling all along.

These strong feelings, motivated my every waking hour, and were engraved in my psyche as life-changing experiences during my early childhood in South Korea.

Once when I was in middle school, and standing in line to buy a bus ticket, a Buddhist nun came up to me and grabbed my hand. "Oh, your hands are like Guanyin, the Goddess of Love." They told my destiny was that of the Bodhisattva, Guanyin.

Although my early life was far from being the life of a Goddess, I didn't dismiss her vision. Even in the midst of my saddest and sickest years, I often felt immersed in a clear bright light, protected by a veil of love. I had no idea what this was and I didn't question it. But at times, when I was growing up, I would find myself engulfed in the brightest, clearest light imaginable. Even though I had many experiences with these lights, I didn't understand their significance. I had no clue that these were cosmic experiences of any kind. But in the midst of a life filled with darkness, these unexplained experiences were clues to life's spiritual possibilities.

Another time, about the same age of puberty, I was reading a book in the flower garden outside of my classroom. I was so absorbed in the story of "Quo Vadis," I didn't notice it was getting dark, but as I finished the book, I looked around and saw it was 9:00 p.m. I did not understand how I had been reading in the black of the night without any artificial lighting. But to my eye, each page was lit up as if I was sitting under a hundred-watt bulb or a flashlight was shining down on it. This still remains a mystery to me.

Later, when I was about 17, I was again reading at school. Heavily engrossed in the Bible, I became totally absorbed in the words of wisdom. I can still feel my deep longing for the truth and passion it inspired. In a flash, I heard a loud voice coming from overhead, like a tremendous Om sound and suddenly, everything was lit up and I couldn't see or read anything. This brightness blocked out any other vision and I felt like I was inside the sun. This was the first time I ever experienced this. Years later, I would experience everything becoming emblazoned in light whenever I intensely focused on finding the truth, or some answers to a confusing world. This intense light brought peace and comfort, even when I didn't understand its significance.

These cherished childhood memories, deeply ingrained in me, have brought me joy and understanding during the turbulent years of my life, even though I slightly remember the day-to-day incidences of ordinary life. I have often reasoned that everything else in my life was so disinteresting and mundane compared to these vivid experiences, I could hardly give credence to their existence.

As I grew and moved on, similar, intense experiences continued throughout my life. Once, when I was working very hard as a realtor in Los Angeles, I remember pulling over to the side of the road because I had heard a loud "Om" resonate throughout my being and the road began to transform into a scene filled with majestic red rocks. It was as if I was in two different places at once; on one hand, I was a realtor driving down a city street in Los Angeles, and on the other, I was in nature among red rocks, mountains and green trees. Not only was I in two different places at the same time, but also the loud "Om" rang inside my head like the inside of a Tibetan singing bowl. Everything was lit up and a brilliant light engulfed my vision.

It took some time before I was able to continue driving, but I wasn't disoriented. Indeed, I had never felt such clarity and I didn't want to move or break the magic of the moment. At that time I didn't know what was happening to me, since my spiritual understanding was underdeveloped. I felt that these "spells" were inconvenient. I was just working so hard to survive and I didn't have the wherewithal to see their incredible value. I was in poor health, without enough energy to barely sustain myself to get through a day, much less interpret these intense experiences.

After the Kundalini energy came, I was able to see these episodes differently. Even though they lasted all day for many days, I didn't see them as inconvenient. Instead, I saw they had special meaning and were, in fact, the bearers of premonitions. For example, the red rocks and green trees from that one experience in Los Angeles were to eventually become my actual home in Sedona, Arizona, fifteen years later.

In Sedona, I continued to hear the same prophetic words from different people. Sedona is a mecca for healers, psychics, channelers, and people with spiritual pursuits and interests. There have been numerous times, when someone would walk up to me on the street and tell me that they saw Guanyin in me.

Once, I stopped by a friend's house, while a well-known channeler from the San Francisco Bay area was giving a reading. As I walked through the door, the channeler stopped what she was saying and turned to me, looked into my face intently and said, "Oh, you are Guanyin." I burst into laughter, as once again someone recognized me out of nowhere as Guanyin. Then she repeated herself with a firm and even louder voice adding, "Do not deny yourself."

In Sedona, I met many psychics and healers, but one I recall in particular. She was asked to my friend's home, and I was one of the guests invited to have dinner with her. Later, I learned that most of the guests were either known psychics or some kind of healers. At this luncheon, this woman told me, "You are a messenger of God, the Goddess of Love, and all your longings will come true." She smiled and added, "Your longing for God is so intense and I can feel it in my heart." Previously, I might have burst into laughter, but this time I burst into tears of relief and joy, because someone had finally recognized and affirmed my intense longing for God and the Truth.

Over the years these kinds of incidents continued to occur. Guanyin was a major theme in my life, and when the Kundalini Energy, the Shakti, bloomed in full force, I started to recognize myself as the Goddess. As my meditations became effortless, I started to see this embodiment with inner eyes.

This was profound because I was experiencing physically and energetically what Guanyin was supposed to feel like.

This meditative state is different from any other feelings. It is the sensation of Peace, Grace, Pure Bliss and Beauty, the very embodiments of Love. Seeing with inner eyes, I was able to witness the energetic grid system beyond the physical body. In this state, I was able to experience the God within that I had once only heard about.

Even though I had many, many of these experiences in America and even early on in South Korea as a child, I was still surprised when, once again, people saw me as Guanyin, this time in India. With so many devotees, worshippers, saints, sages, nuns and monks, I did not expect to stand out in any way. However, time and time again, I met individuals who helped me recognize and remember my true self.

In Rishikesh, a town in the foothills of the Himalayan Mountains in Northern India, I met Shanti Mai, an American woman with blonde hair. I learned she had been working in a fish factory on the west coast of America, when she took time off to travel to India, where she met her Guru. He asked her to stay and become a spiritual teacher and so, of course, she did.

One of the many American travelers I met told me about her gatherings on the shores of the Ganges River. It sounded like a fun and interesting thing to do, so I went. Shanti Ma had everyone chant the "Gayatri Mantra" before guiding us into meditation. Afterwards, she walked over to me and handed me a japa mala strung with one hundred eight rudraksha beads and a pretty pearl at the center. She said, "I have had this mala for a long time, traveling everywhere with it, but I want you to have it. Also, you should come and visit Maharaji at the Ashram." I thought to myself, "What a sweet gift!" And since I knew it was rare for a known saint to just walk up to someone and give him or her such a gift, I felt truly honored.

I met Shanti Mai again the very next day, when I was getting ready to leave Rishikesh. In my preparation to leave, I hadn't thought of her suggestion to see Maharaji. But when I was passing by the Ashram to get a Rickshaw and leave town, I saw Shanti Mai looking out her window, waving her arms and beckoning me to come in. She welcomed me into her room and asked an assistant to bring me a cup of chai. Then she bluntly said, "You are the Goddess of Love and you and I come from the same frequency. When you are out in the world, even if you don't agree with everyone, you need to love them all. Can you do that?"

I wasn't paying much attention to what she was saying, since I was captivated by my constant meditative state. She asked me again, "Are you going to answer me? Are you going to say yes or no?" I nodded my head affirmatively. She asked me to write to her wherever I went to let her know how I was. She asked if she could give me the initiation of "Gayatri Mantra," and put her hands on top of my head while reciting the entire "Gayatri Mantra." Then she gave me a big smile and asked me to practice the mantra with the rudraksha beads she gave me.

I never saw her again, but her kindness and her words to love everyone stuck in my heart. Truthfully, I didn't feel I had love for anyone, since I was mostly a loner and preferred being away from people. I really had no clue what, "love everyone," meant. I was having these extraordinary spiritual experiences of awakening and love, and yet I didn't feel love for my fellow human beings.

I observed that when my eyes were closed and I was sitting alone in meditation, I experienced love and bliss. But when I went out into the world, those feelings of unconditional love didn't go with me and, in fact, this love for people took a long time to settle in my heart.

I learned that this meditative state comes with a very gentle and familiar "Buddha smile," like the one I had seen on Siddhartha's face as he sat so serenely representing the perfect embodiment of compassion and the persona of love. I knew within me that this image was also the image of Guanyin, the Goddess of Love. If I were to complete my spiritual journey, I had to embody that gentle Buddha state within and without.

At that moment, I understood that my inner world and outer world needed to be integrated. Soon, I met the teacher, Rinpoche, at the Garchen Institute in Chino Valley, Arizona, who helped me see this further. I felt that there was so much vanity in the world and I found it to be a very uninteresting place. I had few interests and on most mornings, I didn't even want to get up. Mostly, though, I told him that I felt I had no compassion in my heart and I was in a state of emptiness. Rinpoche told me that it was very dangerous to live without love in a state of emptiness and he urged me to cultivate compassion towards people. I responded, "I do not like being around people," and he wisely replied, "You do not have to be around people to cultivate compassion. You can sit in a cave alone and practice compassion."

This whole idea of universal love was very challenging to someone like me. I could not understand why so many people, over the years, called me Guanyin or thought I was the universal Goddess of Love. I didn't even like people. I yearned to know how an inner experience of perfect love could evolve into actual human expression towards others. I just didn't feel it was possible. I recall one time when I had to deal with some difficult people and my husband asked me if I wanted to feel compassionate towards them. I quickly answered, "Hell no, why should I? I don't even like people." It didn't occur to me to answer affirmatively.

So the slow process of knowing me has been an unfolding. Each experience has helped peel back the illusion of my ego and allowed me to see my true self. Opening the Healing Center has been an important and vital part of this journey. The resistance I felt towards people was challenged by face-to-face encounters in my day-to-day business as a healer. At last, I had to accept that compassion had to be cultivated, not just for some, but for everyone.

The initial years at the Healing Center were a time of introspection and witnessing. I practiced the yoga of relationships and I witnessed my reactive thoughts and emotions. Eventually, I began to notice a shift in my feelings; I was experiencing love toward the world.

It took some time, but during those learning years, a large assortment of clients came to see me and each one taught me a valuable lesson that helped me to grow. The "mean" client taught me patience and how to silently witness what arises within. The "saintly and inspiring" clients showed me examples of what was possible. I practiced compassion with great focus and commitment and it became a more and more recognizable and integral part of me. In time, I began to notice that I could practice it effortlessly.

Love towards my teachers was the easiest and the biggest help. Whenever I needed strength, I would rely on them and their words gave me the confidence I needed when times were difficult. I will always remember my beloved teacher, Robert, and his affirmation of my True Self. A devotee once asked him, as she looked at a picture of Guanyin, "Who is that?"

Robert simply pointed his finger at me. Since she still did not understand the connection, Robert kept looking back and forth at me and then to her and just gave a big smile.

To some this might seem like a meaningless incident, but for me, as I was starting to experience the embodiment of Guanyin, it was life transforming. At that moment, something shifted and I had an acknowledgement and an affirmation. I smiled back at Robert with an understanding few else could appreciate. This was like the Buddhist Flower Sermon, when the disciple, Mahakashyapa, understood his teacher's lesson from the mud encrusted lotus flower, even though no words were spoken. I also understood what Robert meant without his having to do more than smile. And like the story, I gave Robert a "Mahakashyapa smile" and we shared the wordless insight into my true self.

The Goddess of Love was coming out very slowly. Integrating my inner experiences and becoming the expression of compassion took about fifteen years.

During this process, I felt such knowledge flowing into me from my direct experiences. All the mysteries of the religions and spiritual paths started to make sense and I felt I was finally getting answers to all my questions. With the fulfillment of my longings for God, I began to taste the Bliss. Treasures were waiting to be discovered within, for this was the beginning of true purification.

As this spontaneous meditative state came, I saw with an inner eye, that very gentle smile, the "Buddha smile." As I witnessed this perfect and indestructible energy body, I realized that this was the diamond body that Tibetan Buddhism referred to. I was confident that this image was also that of Guanyin, the Goddess of Love.

All of my teachers, my clients, acquaintances and business associates, have led me to this place where I now see what was told to me many years ago and was repeated throughout my life. I see Guanyin manifest in my very self and I am witnessing and experiencing all that I was told. I now know that I am the Goddess of Love and I am confident in my affirmations. And so, I have been able to cultivate and practice compassion with everyone, as I enter the gates of spiritual unfoldment that I always knew existed.

Runaway Bride

"Wanting to reform the world without discovering one's true self is like trying to cover the world with leather to avoid the pain of walking on stones and thorns. It is much simpler to wear shoes."
-*Ramana Maharshi*

"You don't have to be so smart," my eldest brother snarled as he walked by me while I studied on our veranda. "We're going to find you a husband after high school so all this studying is a waste of time." Then he kicked my book out of my hands.

As papers flew to the floor, I was overwhelmed by his cruelty and unconcern for my wellbeing. As a relatively smart and highly motivated young woman, I expected to go to the best university that Korea had to offer. I hoped and prayed my family would have the funds because I certainly had the drive. A scholarship might even be offered to me if I could continue excelling in my studies. My eldest brother's brutality, insensitivity, and male chauvinistic attitudes devastated me at the time and continued to haunt me throughout my young adulthood.

I think at that instant all of my dreams of what I could accomplish and what I might become was shattered. The infinite possibilities that had once been part of my imagination were crushed like little earthworms under a giant's foot.

In a way my brother was correct. In Korea back then, most marriages were arranged through professional matchmakers. Families took great interest in arranging the best "match" they could for their daughters, sisters, and other female relatives. An education beyond high school was not necessary. Even though I received a scholarship to a Christian college to become a minister, my brothers shoved that idea aside.

Unexpectedly one day, a prominent matchmaker delivered a message from a Korean man who had immigrated to America. Now, years later, he had returned to Korea to find a bride. The matchmaker showed his picture to my family and we all noticed that he was extremely good looking, a quality highly sought after by Korean girls. This man had seen me in church and asked about me. When he learned that not only was I attractive to him, but also highly intelligent and well capable, he arranged for the matchmaker to make the initial introduction.

He accompanied the matchmaker to my family's home, seeking approval for "the match." My brother noticed some of his prominent feature and said, "His eyes are like burning fires; this could mean that he has a violent streak." His knuckles were enlarged which indicated to my brother that he had the potential to be an athlete. None of this made any difference to me because of his intense good looks. He also had the ability to take me far away from my hometown and show me the world.

My family approved. I was too young to understand what this really meant, except that I knew that I would be leaving my mother and my life in Korea forever. My mother lovingly tried to make the best of the situation. She knew there was no life for an illegitimate child, especially a girl, in Korea. She knew that my only chance for a successful life would lie in escaping Korea and becoming a bride. She spent the last of her savings to plan a celebration for her daughter's wedding ceremony. Cooking for days, she attempted to bring joy into the arranged marriage. She dreamt and imagined a better life for me, her precious daughter, far across the Pacific Ocean.

As the day approached, her constant tears confused me. They seemed to appear at the slightest provocation. Was she happy with my marriage or was she not? Knowing that she was sending me away to a foreign country and understanding that there was a good chance we might never see each other again, caused her great sadness. She was pleased with the match. The prospective groom was handsome and he had money. She invited friends and neighbors to help her prepare as she worked for days; cooking, cleaning, decorating and bursting into tears often.

I finally arrived in North America, landing in North Carolina where I began my new life as a "bride," not only to the groom but to his entire family as well. Everything was new and overwhelmingly strange. My new family, the new country and all the expectations were incredibly hard to adjust to. I did not know what to expect at any moment. My first impressions of my husband-to-be and his family were not good. It was a setting filled with drama. I moved in with my future husband, mother-in-law, brother-in-law and sister-in-law for a short time. Soon, I moved into a small, dark and dingy apartment with my mother-in-law and husband-to-be.

When I arrived in America, I hit the ground running. Within days I was taught how to drive and because my English was better than most immigrants, I passed the driver's license test on the very first try. The family suggested that I enroll in cosmetology school, which I soon learned was the accepted route for most Asian girls. Running a hair or nail salon was a better option than working at a laundry. I found myself attending cosmetology school and learned I was eventually expected to be the family breadwinner.

They had my future all planned and worked out. There was even worse in store for me. I was shocked by the psychotic behavior of my future groom and his mother. Living in the tiny apartment, there was no sense of privacy at all. They yelled at each other constantly. Screaming at each other was the only way they knew how to communicate. No one was happy or at peace. Once I found my mother-in-law banging her head on the wall in frustration. I assumed she did not like living in America due to the language barriers and cultural differences, but at times it seemed like much more than that.

My husband, her son, also exhibited strange and unacceptable behaviors. Constantly jealous and suspicious, he was always searching my clothing and belonging for evidence of treachery. Several times a day, I would find him sniffing my clothes, questioning my whereabouts and looking through the few personal belongings I had. Once, he found a business card in my handbag. Before I could explain the card's presence, he punched the nearest wall in fury, causing great damage. I remembered my brother's observation, "His eyes are like burning fires."

Within a month I knew that I was living in a hell-hole. With great clarity, I understood that I was imported to be a slave bride to this family. Running a hair salon, driving the car, interpreting the language, cleaning and cooking were all to be part of my wifely duties. There would not be any freedom to be my own person. There was no possibility for me to find happiness under these circumstances.

One evening, while my mother-in-law and my future husband were arguing, I sorted through the medicine cabinet desperately seeking to end my misery. I could see no other way to end my utter despair. I found a bottle of pills and despite not knowing what they were, I poured all the pills into a small bowl. Clutching the bowl of pills tightly, I took them outside and sat in the car, swallowing them all one by one, hoping that relief from my misery would arrive soon.

Waking up in the hospital the next morning, I knew that somehow I had to leave this psychotic mother and her angry son. One morning, not too long after I was released from the hospital, rather than go to cosmetology school, I drove to the Greyhound bus station. I used my budgeted lunch money to buy a ticket to a random destination.

Leaving the car keys under the seat, I boarded a greyhound bus bound for Phoenix,

Arizona. I possessed no money or toothbrush, nothing but the clothes on my back. It took two days to arrive in Phoenix. While riding out to Arizona on the Greyhound bus, a fellow passenger had told me the YWCA was a good place to find help, so I asked someone to take me to YWCA. When I explained my unique circumstances to the staff they introduced me to a family who offered me room and board. It was the opportunity to begin a completely new life!

My life changed dramatically one day when I went along with some friends and took an aptitude test for the Air Force almost by accident. When the Air Force called to tell me that I had high scores on all subjects, it felt as if I had reached the dawn of a new day and all sorts of possibilities were opening up for me. I remember during the swearing in ceremony the feeling of being a part of something greater than myself. I felt that I had been embraced by the greatness of America and would be offered a full range of opportunities that would allow me to reach the fullness of my potential. It was emotionally fulfilling to feel so accepted and I was grateful for the opening of possibilities. I joined the US Air Force and was able to travel the world. During a European tour, I visited England, France, Germany, Belgium, and other countries. While serving in England, I studied Shakespeare and geology. I met many interesting people of various colors and races. Little by little, I began to grow and gain confidence. No longer was I constantly looking over my shoulder to see if the horrific family I escaped from was searching for me.

Eventually, the intense longing for the truth, for God, began to reemerge. While travelling insatiably, I cultivated the feeling that perhaps somewhere I would find the answer to my lifelong question to God, "Where are you?" All alone, I would pray late at night in my room, wherever on the globe it was located.

Constantly searching, I became initiated into Kriya Yoga through the Self Realization Fellowship, as well as Transcendental Meditation. I visited museums and monasteries. I took advantage of all that America and the Air Force could offer in terms of exploration and freedom. After being discharged from the Air Force, I settled in Los Angeles and pursued a career as a stockbroker and realtor. I learned how to live independently even though I still struggled daily with poor health and low energy. Even so, I gave all that I had to pursue the Truth and find the answers that I had sought for so long.

Snow Baba

"Cave is in your heart."
-Robert Adams

India has many pilgrimage sites but the four principal ones, the Char Dham, which consists of Badrinath, Dwarka, Puri and Rameswaram, are considered the goal of every seeker's lifetime. In India, after the visit to Gangotri and Gomuk, I soon found myself headed to Badrinath, following my own inner conviction.

Traveling throughout India was often difficult, part of being a woman but also as a tourist. Mostly because people would want to talk to me, learn my "story," ask me questions. I wanted to be left alone. I was following an inner journey and all the outward expressions of life were of little interest to me. So I shaved my hair and wore only orange pieces of simple cotton cloth. Eventually, I wore a little sign saying that I was in silence.

Once in Badrinath, I stayed in the ashram associated with the temple there and dedicated to Lord Vishnu. The temple is only open six months of the year due to the extreme winter weather and harsh conditions. I was on a mission, though. I had

learned that Snow Baba, an austere and devoted
monk, had a little cave way at the top of a
mountain peak, at the end of a long, arduous and
dangerous climb. Snow Baba was a little monkey
of a man, small and sinewy, living the simple and
frugal life of a monk. Over the many years he lived
at the top of this mountain, only a few had climbed
up to see him. I was determined to be one of these
few; I knew I was special. I knew I would succeed.
I was destined to see his cave and have Babaji's
darshan.

The climb up the 45-degree mountain was
everything that it was rumored to be. On both
sides, the drop below was life-threatening. Up the
icy path all day I hiked until I got to the mouth of
the most charming and beautiful cave. The
entrance was lined with cow dung that had been
transformed into velvet. At the end of the cave was
a perfectly shaped rock bed.

I fell to my knees crying tears of joy and
desire. This was the cave I had dreamed about all
my life. This is where I needed and wanted to be,
where no one would talk to me, where no one
would ask me where I belonged. As I cried, I felt a
hand on my back. A young English boy, Babaji's
translator, said, "Babaji says, 'You can stop crying
now. We are going to find your cave.' Here, come
with me."

The young boy led me to Babaji and I sat humbly before him. He poured me a cup of chai and we faced each other. I knew Snow Baba did not speak English but he could read my heart; he didn't need me to speak. In that moment, I calmed down and knew, deep in my heart, that Babaji would find me the solitude, the cave that I needed. After all, I had found him and succeeded where so many others had not.

With this confidence, I decided to climb further up the mountain in a different direction. I wanted to experience another sacred peak. It took me more than half a day to get high enough to be at the bottom of the sacred peak. It has been said anyone who crossed this line never came back. I knew from there on was a celestial realm. Suddenly I stopped. I was totally engulfed by a mist of clouds. I felt that if I took one step in any direction, I would be sucked into eternity and never return. All the hairs on my body stood up as this current coursed throughout my body.

I could feel Babaji's energy at the top of this mountain, deep in the swirl of the clouds. Faster and faster they swirled around me. I could hear the sound of the clouds moving very fast. The clouds were so thick they hid the snow-capped mountain in front of me.

I watched mesmerized as the clouds started to gather together and formed the flowers of a garland, one by one. I had never seen anything like it. I was frozen in awe. I felt the electricity running throughout my body was getting more intense. In delicate formation, the flowers of the garland came perfectly together. "This is more than coincidence!" I thought. "Babaji is giving me a sign that he heard my cry!" The garland necklace was completely finished and stayed that way for about an hour. I felt strong emotions of love and gratitude rising within me. Then I heard another swishing sound of wind, accompanied by the words, "It is time to go." Soon the garland started to move very fast as if someone was stirring up the air and covered this sacred peak with clouds. This snowcapped mountain peak is usually covered with clouds and very seldom is seen like that. I believe that perfect garland necklace over the peak was the first time.

I knew I had many hours to hike before I returned to the town of Badrinath and the ashram where I was staying. If I didn't leave right that minute, I might never make it down. When I reached the foothills, it was dark. I had made it down just in time. Charged with energy and love, I knew that Babaji had heard me and had answered my prayers.

Korean Nun

"A man of knowledge attains peace only through renunciation."
-Mahatma Gandhi

My trips to India resulted in so many amazing experiences; I want to share several of them for the sheer joy of repeating them. I want the crux of the story, which is the love, to shine through so I ask that I not be held to exact dates.

On one of my journeys, I decided to live in the Himalayan town of Gomuk, which is situated at the mouth of the Ganges River. At this altitude of 3,042 meters, or about 10,000 feet, the air is crystal clean and the water gushing forth from the glacier, which literally looks like a mouth, is pure and clear. Gomuk is a good day's journey from Gangotri, a major pilgrimage spot. It is here that the Goddess Ganges transformed herself into a river to dissolve the sins of King Bhagirath's forefathers, centuries before.

To get to Gomuk from Gangotri, I had to hike many difficult miles, beyond the tree line, where the oxygen level was quite low. I had originally stayed in Gangotri for a while, but I decided to journey to a more pristine area with fewer people. I was hoping to find a cave and perhaps solitude in Gomuk. Walking through the steep hills and mountain trails was truly a dangerous affair. If I made one wrong step, I could have fallen thousands of feet straight down into an isolated and treacherous canyon, and go on to the next life. I also hiked with my own cooking supplies because I only ate the simplest of foods that I personally prepared. My main diet was kitchari, which consisted of rice, dahl, ghee and local veggies if I could find any. I walked with a tiny gas stove and a pressure cooker. Whenever I stopped, I bought whatever ingredients I needed, if they were available, lit my gas stove, and mixed everything in the pressure cooker. Although this food was very delicious and truly the only way I could survive, it was a very mundane and dull diet. Consequently, when I met a new friend, who could make magic out of any ingredient, I couldn't believe my good fortune.

I was living in Gomuk, in a little hut I rented very close to the glacier mouth of Ganga. I shopped for local vegetables at the little street market. One day, I met a Korean nun. She was wearing a simple gray Buddhist monk robe and donned a gray hat that covered her shaved head. You can imagine how surprised we both were to see another Korean in the high Himalayan Mountains. We immediately became friends and I invited her to stay in my hut while she was in Gomuk.

This dear nun stayed with me for ten days, and these ten days are some of the most memorable of my life. It seemed like we had known each other forever. The first night we stayed up all night telling each other pilgrimage stories. When I invited her to partake of my Kitchari, she smiled sweetly and showed me one of her most outstanding talents. She could cook a gourmet meal out of almost nothing! And she put my pressure cooker to shame.

For example, one day she found a discarded can rolling around in town. To anyone else, this would be seen as garbage, plain and simple, but not to my friend. Flattening out the can, she used a nail she found in the road and pounded out indentations. Then she found four small wooden sticks and tied them expertly together to make it sturdy. With this "tool" she grated potatoes by rubbing them up and down the indented can. That night we had potato pancakes fried in ghee, an exciting meal anywhere. When we found turnips and peppers a different day, she made the Korean national dish, kimchi, by setting the ingredients in the sun to ferment. Who would have thought?

She cooked gourmet and we talked about God all night long. She was such a special friend. When

I asked how she began her pilgrimage journey, she graced me with her story.

She had been living in a temple as the female senior monk. The owner of the monastery, who was the head nun, wanted to retire due to her age, and suggested that my friend take her position and manages the monastery as head nun. Although it was an honor to be offered such a role, my friend thought differently. She reasoned, "I left my mundane life, my family, and my career to find Enlightenment. Why should I drop that search to get involved, once again, in ordinary responsibilities? I choose not to." And she didn't. She left the temple and began her pilgrimage, eventually finding herself making kimchi in my little hut in Gomuk.

Once she made us lassie. This delicious fermented milk drink needs to be blended. I watched with great curiosity as she went outside to look for a particular branch of a pine tree. She needed a branch with five nodules coming out of one section. She cut and polished the branch with the five nodules and then took it and placed it in the fermented milk. Using her hands, she rubbed back and forth, creating a makeshift blender. Ingenious, huh?

At that time, as I recall, I had very long hair. It was such beautiful hair, dark and thick, that it became a distraction in so many ways. People would comment on my hair and want to touch it. I didn't want to be known as the lady with the hair, so I decided to cut it. This was a daunting task in the high mountain of Gomuk.

My Korean nun friend volunteered to do the cutting. She told me that she had never wanted to cut a female monk's hair because she didn't want to be responsible for something so potentially huge in one's life.

"You, however, are a real monk," she told me, "And so I would be pleased to cut your hair." I sat down and she lovingly cut my thick locks, and shaved it all off, while she performing a little ceremony with prayer. The change in my appearance was like night and day. I was happy with the change, however, and I kept that lock of hair for years. Just recently, I donated that lock to "Lock of Love," a cancer victim's hair donation center. As for the grater and the blender, I still have them among my most treasured possessions.

On the day that my dear friend cut my hair, I celebrated the event by walking to a big cave and taking a ceremonial dip where the water from the Ganges rushes out with unbelievable energy. It was mostly ice cubes floating, while underneath that layer, brilliant, sparkling water rushed forth. The energy was so intense and so pure; I just sat by the mouth of the cave and sobbed like a child. On the rare occasion that I took a bath in that icy water, pain would shoot all over my body from the intense cold.

We were, sitting at the water's edge, looking down river, settling in with the feeling of my bald head, when we spotted a Korean male monk and an older lady walking up the river. We were stunned, as it had been so long since we had spoken to anyone, especially Koreans, like ourselves. Our first reaction was to walk quickly back to our hut, close the door and hide.

We were surprised when we heard a knock on the door. Hesitantly, we opened the hut's door. There stood the monk we had seen at the river. He was as amazed as we were. He had no idea that two Korean females with shaved heads would be opening the door to his request for water. But there we were, two Korean women, monks if you will, without hair, practicing meditation at the top of the mountains in India, and crossed path with them!

The lady with him was his sister and they were taking a pilgrimage. He was so moved that as they were leaving Gomuk, he left us with a case of ramen noodles and a big box of dried fruits and nuts. Both these items were a king's treasure up in the high Himalayan mountaintops. He also left us with a stainless steel thermostat. My nun friend was so creative when it came to cooking on the road that she turned those ingredients into gourmet meals. We made so many dishes out of this ramen noodle; ramen spaghetti, ramen soup, ramen salad, etc. We experienced such abundance out of nowhere; we were feasting on top of that mountain.

My nun friend did not have an address and I didn't even know her by her formal name. When she left Gomuk, she said she was heading to Nepal, but there was no way for us to keep physical contact. Instead, we have kept in contact heart to heart. I have so many loving memories of her and I still possess the grater and the blender along with her beautiful stories. I hope to meet her again someday.

Lakshmana Swami

"God, Guru and Self are one and same."
-Lakshmana Swami

Arunachala means "red hills," and is the birthplace of Ramana Maharishi. Ramana Maharishi's energy is so powerful that it continues to influence many beings to extinguish their final veil and reside in the state of self-effulgence permanently. Two of my teachers, Papaji and Robert, have both met Ramana in person, and carried the lineage of Ramana Maharishi, known as Advaita Vedanta.

Ramana, himself, had a spontaneous awakening at the age of 16 after facing the death of his uncle, with the self-inquiry of, "Who am I?" Afterwards, he went to Arunachala and sat in a cave for eighteen years, known as Virupaksha cave. Currently, it is a pilgrimage spot for many seekers.

I vividly remember sitting in this cave all day sobbing, purging and going through boxes of tissues. The energy was extremely intense in this cave. I experienced many amazing things here. But of all the beautiful stories of Arunachala, my encounter with Lakshmana swami is the most unforgettable.

Lakshmana swami was a yogi. With one gaze from Ramana Maharishi, he was awakened to the radiance of the heart. The story of Lakshmana is quite beautiful, and I would like to tell of my encounter with Lakshmana swamiji.

When I arrived in town, I learned he only gave darshan once a year, and did not appear to people, I was told. His house was surrounded by a large garden with tall trees and concrete walls. It seemed impossible to get a glimpse of this saint unless one was invited. I decided to stay in Arunachala for another month, so I could be there for his scheduled darshan day, which was in early November of that year. For me, seeing a saint would be one of the most interesting events of my journey, and something that really seemed to matter.

My expectation and excitement grew as each new day brought me closer to that event. I wanted to somehow prepare myself, because in those days I would drop into meditation at any moment, anywhere. Sometimes, it would be on a doorstep, at a chai stall, on the street, or in a restaurant. I was concerned that I might not be able to stand or, even be conscious after receiving swami's darshan. So I asked an Indian woman I met to accompany me, just in case, I were to fall into that state of meditation or Samadhi, and she could carry me out.

Finally the day came and the front gate of swami's house swung open. There were only twenty of us waiting for this moment, and I sat in front of everyone. The door of the house opened, and swamiji, in a white punjabi outfit, came out and sat directly in front of me. I remember he said only one sentence. "God, Guru, Self are the same." His eyes swept over everyone, pausing for a moment to look directly at me. His energy was very intense and my heart seemed to stop. I felt like I was immersed in white light, as though I had walked into living moonlight. Perhaps I was having a heart attack, since his frequency was so high; it stirred up any impurities I was holding onto. In retrospect, I think I could have died, because I was barely surviving in the swami's frequency like being in a frying pan. Very quickly, swami got up and walked back into his house. I felt so disappointed, realizing only a few minutes had passed. I could not say a word, since everything had stopped inside of me. Inwardly, I screamed repeatedly, "Please come back, please come back. Stay longer."

Swamiji, who was still at the door, suddenly turned as if he heard me. He walked back, grabbed a chair, sat in front of me close, and stared into my eyes. Oh Lord, it is true! A saint can hear thoughts from your heart! He heard my heart scream, and came back to fulfill this poor girl's wish. He sat there for about five minutes with so much intensity! I was lifted into white light and immersed in pure radiance, even though I was having tightness in my heart, and could not breathe. His frequency was able to lift me to that "Sat, Chit, Ananda;" Pure Awareness, Pure Consciousness, Pure Bliss. Inside, I was stunned by this ecstatic beauty, witnessing this vast pure light. If I had to die then, I could not have been any happier. Of course, my body turned into a noodle, and I vaguely remember my Indian lady friend lifting me up and carrying me out as prearranged. She had to stop many times before we were able to get back to the ashram although it was only about 100 feet away from the swami's house. I stayed in this state for a week. The contact with Lakshmana swami I made is eternal. Whenever I reminisce about those moments, I can transfer to that beautiful state. The fact he heard my wish and turned around was a confirmation that if one's heart's desire is one hundred percent, it will be heard by God, Consciousness.

The love I had for his grace, and the sensations I experienced were a witness to the eternal. I will always hold onto that moment of intensity thanking God for giving me that rare opportunity to meet and have the darshan of a self-realized saint. I felt fortunate, thinking perhaps God had not forsaken me, after all.

Narayan Swami

"Like Space,
Meditate without Centre or limit!
Like the Sun and the Moon,
Meditate in brightness and clarity!
Like the Mountains,
Meditate unmoving and unshakable!
Like the Ocean,
Meditate deep and unfathomable!"
-Milerapa

While in Arunachala, an Indian family
invited me to join them on their visit to see
Narayan swami, who lives at the top of
Arunachala. I had heard of this swami before.
Narayan swami, known as a breatharian, does not
eat or sleep. I had seen pictures of him when he
was meditating in the cave, looking like a skeleton.
I had many thoughts of visiting him, and now
finally I met an Indian family who came regularly
to visit Narayan swami and receive his blessings.
"This is the opportunity I have been waiting for!" I
thought.

They always left before dawn, a little before
four am, so I woke up early to meet the whole
family in the courtyard of the ashram. It would

take about four hours of climbing the mountain to where swami lived. This was not easy for my weak constitution; however, I was determined to meet Narayan swami, so, I made it to the top of the hill.

The swami was inside a little ragged shack-like tent. I recalled that people said he never looked at anyone directly because his energy was so intense, most people couldn't handle his gaze. I asked the Indian family why this was and they replied, "His frequency is so high, it brings everyone's negativity quickly to the surface. Some people might go mad, or others might just die instantly."

Now my curiosity increased. "What is the point of climbing up the mountain without getting his real darshan, his gaze?" I decided there and then, "I am not going down this hill until I see his face!"

There were many people already lined up by the time I arrived. All had gotten there early in the morning for swami's darshan. At this time, I was bald without a hair on my head and I was dressed as a wandering sadhu, wrapped in orange cloth. Each person received a little cup of tea and half a piece of banana as prasad (blessed food). After climbing this mountain for four hours, this was all people received. Again, I was impressed with Indian devotion. However, since I am Korean and stubborn, I would not be satisfied without his darshan. They might be satisfied with tea and banana, but I had to see his face.

I was at the end of the line trying to figure out how to get to the front to look at his face, I noticed a small side little entrance to the humble shack, made of brushes and weeds and only about 20 square feet. Then something magical happened. One of the chella; who monitors the darshan, pointed his finger at me and said, "You come here, sit at the front."

My heart lit up as I thought, "Somebody is listening to me!" I passed all the people in line and sat in front of the little entrance to the shack. I could see him sitting in a squat position. He was very skinny and I could feel a lot of light and vibrant energy surrounding him. His face was covered with a large cone shaped hat made from some kind of flour bag. It was a plastic like cloth shaped to cover his face and most of his front and upper chest. I could only see his feet and the bottom of his hands.

I was determined to see his face. I bent down and lowered myself to the ground in order to sneak a peek into the head covering. The assistant chella, scolded me, saying "You stop that! You must not see swamiji's face."

I waited a little while and then tried again. The chella again pointed his finger at me, ready to yell, but I straightened my body before I heard him speak.

Then the most mystical thing happened. Narayan swami lifted his hat with his right arm and looked straight at me. My heart lit up with surprise. "Wow!" There he was in full form. Then I saw two beams of light coming out of his eyes, and we held our eye gaze for a few seconds. But to my dismay, he once again covered his face with his made-up hat. "Oh no, Not yet, please!" I screamed in my heart. Then he lifted his hat one more time. "Wow! Thank you!" I humbly and silently said.

The communication that occurred during those few moments is truly indescribable. As I fell to the ground, I was swimming in golden light and highly intoxicated. I could not open my eyes for a long time, as I had gone into some other realm.

It was getting late into the afternoon and most people were starting to leave since it was a long way down the mountain. The Indian family who went with me to the mountain was still waiting for me to come out of the condition I was in. But that was impossible since I was swimming in ecstasy. They finally decided to help me up and walk me down the hill, but my body was practically dead weight.

They managed to bring me down to a large cave in the middle of the mountain, where they sat me down while they visited with the swami who was practicing his meditation there. From deep within, I could hear their voices talking about me to the swami. "Who is this woman, who received Narayan swami's darshan? We have been coming to see him for years but never got his darshan. She must be important. We should make a temple for her, and take care of her." Then I felt them kneeling and bowing in front of me. As part of the Indian culture, it is typical for them to worship swamis and meditators. But I was trying to avoid this kind of attention at all costs. That evening after dark, when we finally returned to the ashram, there was a surprise waiting for us. The manager swami was very upset because I was spending my time with Indians and going off with people I didn't know. These Indians were still giving me too much attention by putting me on a pedestal and worshiping me as a Deity. The manager swami's response was so impassioned; he did not seem to cool down any time soon. Uncomfortable with all this commotion coming at me from all directions, I decided to leave.

Gathering all my belongings, I went to the bus station and left Arunachala.

Tiny Baba

"As all creatures come forth from the unseen into this world, so they return to the unseen and so will they come again till they be purified."
-Jesus of Nazareth

Approximately 2.5 miles from Badrinath, a natural rock bridge lies situated near the beginning of a trail that leads to the revered Vasudhara waterfall. This is the legendary bridge that the five Pandhava Brothers crossed in the Mahabharata to ascend to heaven. When you see this bridge, it is obvious that no human could have placed that giant rock across the canyon, creating this bridge. It could only have been a divine miracle. At the beginning of the bridge, there is a giant cave, where the sage Vyasa lived while he wrote the Mahabharata.

As I crossed this bridge, I immediately felt the vibration of the air change. The scenery looked so different and otherworldly, I had the feeling I was entering a heavenly realm; it was so peaceful. Watching the deer grazing on the distant celestial hillside, I thought to myself, "No wonder Indians make this arduous pilgrimage up the Himalayas, only to fall off the cliff believing that they are ascending to heaven!" I was mesmerized by the peace and beauty of the place.

As I walked, my experiences went beyond the earthly realm. I noticed interesting looking trees on steep hills, even though we were above the tree line. An Indian man walking the trail told me that they were papal trees, the ones that sages make paper to write on.

As I walked on this trail with the vastness of the mountain surrounding me, I felt like I was floating on air and shimmering light engulfed me. The air was so pristine, it was beyond human toxicity. Just being there, I felt all negativity wash away. I had heard it said that no negative thoughts were allowed in this sacred place. To aim an arrow at a deer would be risking blindness to the hunter. After a leisurely stroll for a few hours, I arrived at the end of the trail. The story said that anyone going beyond this point would never return, believing that he had actually ascended to heaven, just like the Pandhava Brothers.

Here, there were glaciers and an enormous waterfall. When I looked up at this waterfall, it was like looking up into heaven. It was so high that I couldn't see to the top and imagined that it was one of the tallest waterfalls in the world. As I watched, falling water turned into mist as it hit the bottom with the glacier stretching out below.

Standing there, this mist felt so refreshing and divine, like the kisses of an angel. I stood there for a long time enjoying this awesome sensation, in a shower of blessings.

Then I heard an Indian man say, "There is a cave up there," and I followed him as he climbed the hill. Within a few minutes, we stopped in front of the most beautiful cave ever imaginable. The view from the front of this cave was extraordinary looking out into the vastness of the Himalayas. Suddenly a small man, a tiny Baba, waved as he walked out of the cave.

Smiling, he invited us into the cave where there was a fire pit in the center. He made chai for us and said that he only drank chai, and ate no other food. I reasoned that, since the air was so pure, he could have been a Breatharian. He did not have any possessions except dry milk, tea, a teapot and a few small teacups. What a simple life!

He was small, like a little monkey, but his presence was still and calm. He seemed totally content, living on the vitality and nourishment of the sparkling clean air and water in his native home. The view from his cave gave me the feeling that this is what it would look like if one could look down from heaven. You would see mountain peaks and clouds swirling around other peaks. It was so vast! Sitting in that celestial cave, drinking chai, I wondered, "Where is my cave? What do I have to do to live in a cave like this?"

Inspired by this most beautiful cave and " tiny Baba", I planned it all out in my head to live a simple life in this heavenly realm while designing my beautiful cave. I upgraded my cave with beautiful views, a nice door and a window including a flower garden at the front porch. I wondered if this intense desire to live in the cave was reminiscent of some past life. I kept having flashes of memories living in a cave, practicing meditation with intense devotion and desire for liberation. It always felt that a cave life was my true home. Someone said I was burning out my "shankalpa," which means "innermost longing and desire." I envied this "tiny Baba" who enjoyed life untouched by human civilization. If I could vote for the most beautiful cave in the world, this cave by the celestial water fall with an indescribable view would be my choice. I imagine that the Pandhava brothers enjoyed this view with a cup of chai before they ascended to heaven. Perhaps this *is* the heavenly realm and they are still here but I just don't see them with my physical eyes.

After staying in the Himalayas for six months and dreaming of my own cave, I decided to go down to Rishikeshi for supplies and rupees. I would have loved to have stayed at the edge of

Badrinath full-time if I could, but non-natives require a special permit to do so. The living conditions in the winter were so difficult that it was believed that only the most dedicated native could live there. Individuals lived on powdered milk and flour and had to supply their own wood throughout the harshest weather. I thought to myself that I should apply for this permit, as I was pretty sure I would be one of the few non-natives who would get permission to stay year round.

So, I went to my usual hot springs bath at the foot of Badrinath peak and later headed down to the Rishekeshi. While getting supplies and rupees, I saw a poster of "Aja," meaning Grandpa, who was a saint living in Mangalore near Bangalore. That same day I received an email from my friend in America describing "Aja" in length and urging me to go visit him. "Well, so much for my dream cave," I thought as I headed to southern India, to begin the rest of my pilgrimage. I visited Sai Baba, Aja, and Orbindo's Ashram and then on to Andaman Island. It wasn't easy moving around with my two Sitars, stove, pots and large backpack, but it was well worth all the effort. I started to forget about my dream cave. I was being led down a different path, towards a new adventure and I never went up that mountain again.

My Three Teachers

"And the Word was made flesh, and dwelt among us, and we beheld his glory, the glory as of the only begotten of the father, full of grace and truth."
-John 1:14

Although I have had many teachers along the way, I must make special mention of three great beings: Papaji, Robert Adams and Thakar Singh. It may seem rather paradoxical to say that words cannot describe what it is like to be in each of their presences, because that is exactly what I am going to attempt to do. Perhaps it is because being in "love" cannot truly be described except by the greatest of poets.

But how does a humble devotee describe her teachers? To be in their presence is like being in the presence of Divine Love, the embodiment of what God must be. On the surface, these great beings may seem like normal people. They laugh, they cry, they joke, eat and sleep much like anyone, yet they are very different and very special. An extraordinary fragrance permeates their physical presence and anyone who comes in contact with them is benefitted. To this day, I am in awe of the kindness and grace they each bestowed upon me when I met them.

Papaji of Lucknow

"Stillness of mind comes from giving up all attachments except that attachment to Self. When the mind is quiet, all is Self. When the mind moves the world arises, so be still, throw away everything, and be free."
-*Papaji*

I lived in Los Angeles, California for about eighteen years, during which time I was very weak and depressed, with extremely low energy. I worked hard to survive and was relatively successful in the eyes of the world. I was a single, minority woman who was a successful realtor and stockbroker. Those years working in Los Angeles taught me many lessons about the world, and in 1990 I was finally led to beautiful Sedona in the red rock high country of Northern Arizona.

As I mentioned in earlier chapter, one day while I was walking along Oak Creek, I fell and landed on my hip, severely damaging my lower back. In retrospect, I believe this was a cosmic event, similar to the falling episodes I had as a young child. I didn't know it then, but this painful physical experience was the precursor to my Kundalini awakening. I was quite innocent at that time, compared to what I now know about spiritual energy and knowledge. After all, in my mind, I was just a hardworking, driven real estate agent, who, for the most part, had given up on the concept of ever finding God and Truth.

I couldn't understand what was happening to me. I couldn't sit or lie down on my back for weeks. The severe damage to my back was explainable, but the incredible energy that coursed throughout my body, day and night, with feather-like feelings intoxicating my every pore, kept me out of commission for about ten years. I had difficulty with everyday living and I became very dysfunctional. Of course, it was inconvenient to not be able to move very well. The energy I felt was putting me into spontaneous meditation and I seemed to be experiencing what it would be like on LSD or something similar. My body would go into strange motions and my hands would form mudras. Dancing, jerking and tilting my head, seeing colors and various visions were part of my day-to-day experiences.

At first, I was worried about how I would live and function in the world. However, as time passed, I began to feel unconcerned about daily matters. My spontaneous meditations felt too wonderful for me to worry about paying bills or dealing with day-to-day issues.

Later, when I began studying in India, at the Kagyu International Buddhist Institute in Delhi (KIBI), I learned that my experience was "textbook" for a Kundalini awakening. This includes the rise of spiritual energy through the chakras, alongside the spine and running to the top of the head and even beyond. This went on for several years. When I couldn't move, sitting in meditation, my day-to-day life was miraculously taken care of by special individuals, who just showed up and began to lovingly look after me.

Eventually, one of my close friends brought me to a lady who had explored and studied many eastern religions. She, too, had visited several saints before and when we met, she urged me to go to India and find Papaji. She looked me deep in the eyes and said, "My sister, who loves God so much, this is beautiful. You are just a simple realtor and you do not know anything of this nature." I still remember her beautiful blue eyes dripping tears like dew drops from a flower. Over the years, this woman has helped me, guided me and protected me. What a spiritual friend! Once, when I was in India, she collected the rent from my rental property in Sedona and actually came to India to give me the money, so that I could live there longer. If she wasn't able to bring the money, she made sure that others, who were traveling to

India, would bring it to me as she would. In other words, she made sure I had enough money to survive.

After I received Papaji's address, I was guided to go, without knowing much about where I was going or whom I was going to see. I felt compelled to go to India and knew it was the right thing to do, even with my uncertainty.

In the spring of 1995, I landed in India around 11:00 p.m. As I walked off the plane, I could feel that India was truly magical. There was instant cultural shock as I took in the many sights at the airport. The smells, sights, sounds and feelings of India were all vivid and exciting. Nothing was familiar yet it felt like home. I expected to find my way to a hotel, but suddenly I realized I had no idea how to go about it. I didn't speak the language and I was shy about communicating in English.

Looking around, I noticed the most beautiful woman wearing a colorful sari. I was in awe of her loveliness and grace. She must have noticed how out of place I looked, or maybe she saw the awe in my face as I took in her divine beauty. She smiled at me and asked me where I was headed. I told her that I was going to see Papaji in Lucknow but wanted to find a hotel for the night. She said, "No, no hotel. Come with me. Stay with me. I am here to pick up my son who is flying in from England. Come to our house, have dinner with us and stay the night."

In the car, with her and her son, I looked out into the streets to the most amazing sights! I smelled those streets with their strange food odors and cows and yet I could feel a powerful spiritual energy throughout the country. But so many cows all over the streets! I laughed and laughed, watching the cows "own" the road and blocking traffic. I could tell right away that, indeed, Indians worshipped their cows.

This wonderful woman made me feel like a long lost sister. She took my hand and led me to their home, where we spent the night feasting and talking. She invited me to stay longer, but I said that I was eager to visit Papaji. The next morning, she sent her son with me to the train station to make sure I got on the right train. Then, he directed the conductor to protect and watch over me on the train, and to make sure I woke up at my stop at midnight, found a taxi and even negotiate a fair price. All this, the conductor, a complete stranger, did for me on behalf of this wonderful woman and her son.

When I arrived at Lucknow's train station, the conductor woke me as promised and then I took the taxi he arranged to the Satsang house.

Since it was the middle of the night and I was exhausted and unsure what to do next, I decided to sleep outside the gate. As I settled on the concrete floor to spend the rest of the night, I heard a voice saying, "Did you just get here?" I saw a young man who explained that he had an urge to walk by Papaji's house. He said he heard in his head, "Go to Satsang house." When he saw me, he felt he knew why he was sent. Inviting me home with him, he asked me if I wanted to sleep in his room while he slept outside on a cot.

As we walked into his room, the young man told me his name was Shakshin. He said, "I am a shoemaker and I make shoes for Papaji. Would you like to try a pair on?" As I put the shoes on my feet, the reaction was so intense, I sobbed throughout the night, unable to sleep. The energy was running through my system so strongly that I couldn't function well and I would drift into spontaneous meditation as if I wasn't even there. I cried and cried until morning.

At dawn, something told me I should find some flowers to bring to Papaji. I found a flower shop and bought a bouquet for my first meeting with him. As I walked to Satsang that morning, carrying my flowers, I remember feeling strongly intoxicated. As I walked towards Papaji, I saw lotus flowers under my feet, simply appearing under each foot as I made my way toward the front. Could this be a psychedelic experience like those I had read about?

As a first time visitor, the hall monitor invited me to sit up front. As soon as I sat, I went into spontaneous meditation. Bam! I was gone. I became immobile, frozen. As Satsang ended and it was time for me to give flowers to Papaji, someone pushed me forward and said, "Give him the flowers NOW!" I fell at Papaji's feet. Papaji, himself, reached down and picked me up. My eyes were half closed, rolled up into my head, and I saw Papaji's eyes. They were full of tears. As he wiped the tears from his eyes, he whispered, "Beautiful. Beautiful."

I finally opened my eyes fully and there he was, a Buddha in human form. He was my first Guru, my enlightened master. My longing and dreams of God and all the saints had finally been realized. Every desire to know myself and experience love was contained in his gaze.

Papaji stood up and pulled me to him. He told someone to take a picture of us and then turned and took me to a sitting room adjacent to the Satsang room. He called over a Japanese lady and told her to give me a room, stay with me and care for me. He told her that he wanted daily reports about me and for her to bring me to his house for lunch that day.

I stayed with the Japanese girl as directed. She had been there a long time and I think she might have been jealous of the attention and special treatment I was receiving from Papaji. When our Master sent me prasad (special blessed food) at dinner, I was mostly in a meditative state and couldn't eat. Sometimes, I would notice that the Japanese girl would eat the prasad Papaji meant for me. Then she would put me in a rickshaw that took me to Papaji's house and I would sit there, in meditation, pretty much unaware of my surroundings or good fortune. Papaji would occasionally feed me prasad and give instructions about my care.

I stayed in Lucknow for a few months. It was very intoxicating just being in India in His presence and in the presence of hundreds of other seekers. One time, an Indian man offered to give me a massage. By this time, I was living in Papaji's own guesthouse. While there, Papaji had told an American lady to look after me and report to him everything that happened. She told him about the Indian man and his offer of massage. She said that when Papaji heard that, he screamed, "No one touches her. Don't let anyone touch her." I did not understand any of this at the time, but I suppose now that Papaji was being very protective of me and my experiences.

While I was still in Lucknow, a hunchbacked person befriended me. He was quiet and introverted and most likely found me a kindred spirit. One morning he told me he was going to see a saint who used to be with Neem Karoli Baba and asked me if I would like to come as well.

When we arrived, there were several young Indian people in the room sitting around the saint, K.C. Tewari. As usual, as soon as we sat, I fell into spontaneous meditation and went into Samadhi, totally immobilized. My body took on a death-like appearance with my eyes open that some people thought I had died. Although devotees of this saint had seen many seekers experience intense meditation experiences, this obviously was one of the more extreme. My body went stiff, my eyes remained open and my breathing became soft and low.

The devotees did not understand what was happening to me and became afraid. My hunchbacked friend was also in deep meditation, with his mouth wide open, totally unaware of his surroundings. Overreacting dramatically, the young Indians began to slap my face to bring me back from the dead. When I did not respond, they slapped me harder. Then they started to punch my stomach, thinking they could bring me back from the dead. I was aware of all this, but just could not come out of this state.

Finally, a few Indian boys dragged me from the room to the outdoor water pump. They had the idea to pull on my tongue, while another one held my mouth open. Someone else started punching me aggressively in the stomach and buckets of water were thrown on me. I remember wishing that I could come out of this trance and tell them to stop, but I couldn't. I was tortured and helplessly drenched in water.

By this time, my friend had awakened from his meditation and went looking for me, wondering where everyone had gone. At the same time, Tewari came back from whatever he was doing and saw what was happening to me. He screamed, "Stop! Stop! What are you doing?" He ran and rescued me from that horrible situation. When I was able to move my body, I got into a rickshaw and returned to Papaji's guesthouse. The next day, Papaji told a story about a Korean girl who had cheated on her husband and got into trouble. It was a strange story to everyone but me, for I knew I was the bride and Papaji was the husband and the analogy was meant for me.

I hardly slept while I was in Lucknow because the spiritual energy was so intense and most nights I was in a meditative state. I remember having vivid visions of Ramana Maharishi nightly; experiencing thick transmissions of silence. This darshan experiences were extremely powerful as were other experiences of grace from Papaji I had when I was in Lucknow.

Then, one day at Satsang, Papaji gave me my spiritual name, Chintamani, which means "wish-fulfilling diamond," and then he told the following story:

There once was a great but humble holy man. He travelled far and wide looking for just the perfect person with which to bestow his most valuable possession, a wish-fulfilling diamond. Such an object's value was beyond measure, but what could one do with this wish-fulfilling diamond? Pretty much anything and everything! So, he travelled far and wide, to find just the right person to receive this precious gem.

One day, he met a modest and simple shoemaker in the foothills of the Himalayas and he handed the diamond to the shoemaker, saying, "Here! This is for you." The shoemaker respectfully accepted the gift and politely put it on a shelf in his home. As the years passed, the shoemaker paid little attention to the wish-fulfilling diamond, but just protected it on a high shelf in his humble home.

Before the holy man passed years later, he decided to travel once again to the home of the shoemaker to see what the shoemaker had done with this most remarkable gift. He soon learned that the shoemaker had done nothing with it, having left it on a shelf all those years, unused, untouched, but protected and secure.

As the story came to a close, Papaji called on Shakshin, the young shoemaker, and told him to take care of the new wish-fulfilling diamond, me, Chintamani. When Satsang ended, Shakshin came to me and told me he would like to move in with me. Misunderstanding his intent, and furious that Papaji would expect me to be interested in a man, I dashed off a letter to Papaji. How dare he fix me up with a man I am not interested in! I hadn't come 3,000 miles to be with a shoemaker. I came all this way to be with you! So many thoughts went through my head and I was not afraid to say any of them. Although most seekers do exactly what their Guru commands, I was not one of them. I went my own way and was always independent.

I walked up to Papaji and handed him my letter. His smile was exactly as it always was, full of love and humor. He called Shakshin to him and said, "She doesn't want to be with a man. Go home." And then he laughed and laughed.

I eventually left Lucknow and, as hard as it is to believe, I met up with Shakshin many months later in the large city of Delhi. He was sitting in a coffee shop, and though I'm sure we had both changed very much over that time, we immediately recognized each other. Over chai, my old friend told me, "After all these months, I just have to tell you something. When Papaji told me to take care of you, he also said, "Don't touch her. You can take care of her, but don't ever touch her." Just like the diamond in the story, the shoemaker was to take care of the wish fulfilling diamond, but never touch it.

There are so many, many stories to tell of my time with Papaji, each one filled with meaning and lessons. Papaji lovingly and unimaginably helped me along my spiritual journey. He gave me a foundation of love, but never insisted that I become dependent or attached to him and give up my own free will. I learned that my ultimate goal was to find my own true nature, not through mechanical and unmindful thinking, but through experience and love. I allowed Grace to bless me through my teacher and, indeed, Papaji truly blessed me.

Robert Adams

"There is only one I actually. That I is Consciousness. When you follow the personal I to the source, it turns into the universal I......You do this by keeping quiet. The fastest way to realization is to keep quiet."
-*Robert Adams*

After staying in Lucknow a few months, I went on to Arunachala, Puri and Nepal. I also spent a few months in Delhi attending Kagyu International Buddhist Institute. Eventually, my visit to India ended and I returned to my home in Sedona. Before ever going to India, I had lived with dear friends who cared for me. It may seem strange that as a young woman I would still need to be cared for, but my Kundalini experiences had been so intense that I literally spent most of my time in a Samadhi state, unable to care for my everyday needs. When I returned home from Papaji, these few friends still continued to help me, and at times, they would literally walk me to the bathroom or feed me through a straw. The simplest, most mundane tasks were beyond my abilities, as I remained engulfed in the spiritual world.

I brought home so much from India and my heart was full, but I could barely make sense of what was happening to me. In the midst of all these revelations, I began to see a repeating image. The beautiful visage of a man with large eyes kept appearing before me, whether or not my eyes were open or closed. Since I was used to strange experiences, having so many of them, I just tucked this vision away, as well.

One day, on the rare occurrence that I was awake and aware, my friend showed me a picture of a teacher she saw in Los Angeles. I instantly recognized the face.

"This is the vision I've been seeing day and night! Who is that?" I asked.

My friend told me that his name was Robert Adams and he was a self-realized sage who held a small Satsang in California. However, globally, he was known as a great teacher, whose emanation was similar to that of Ramana Maharishi.

I was so intrigued that when another friend asked me if I wanted to drive out to Los Angeles and meet Robert Adams, I enthusiastically agreed. Somehow, I knew that this meeting, between Robert and myself, was going to be life changing.

I went to Los Angeles living out of my van while I was having Satsang with Robert and borrowing showers from various devotees' houses. I felt Robert's frequency was very pure and beneficial to my spiritual purification. He was very generous with his time and would invite me to eat with him or be with him in the park. Of course, sitting next to him I would very quickly drift off into meditation. It appeared to me that he was in a state of Samadhi all the time. He was here, but not really here. It was that sort of feeling, if you know what I mean.

After a few months, I got tired of living out of my van, so I returned to Sedona. One day my friend from California called and said, "Robert wanted to know where you went, so I told him that you went back to Sedona and he wasn't happy about that." She continued, "You need to call him."

Instead, I wrote a letter to Robert, dictated to a friend, saying, "Robert, Please move to Sedona. We will take care of you."

I told him he could stay in my home and my friends and I would take care of him financially. I was told that, in the past, many people had tried to get Robert to come to their towns, but he never would make any moves. However, in September of 1997, Robert showed up unannounced in Sedona to check out the area. This was such a surprise and soon after this visit, he moved to Sedona. My friend rented him a nice house, while all of his belongings were sent in a moving van. Later, I had the opportunity to drive him from Los Angeles to Sedona in my van with his dog, Dimitri.

Robert's presence was most amazing. His main teaching was basically, "Silence of the heart," and that is what I experienced with Robert, silence. Whenever I was with him, all my dramas, stories, thoughts and impurities would simply be wiped out, as his frequency and vibration were just so pure. However, not everyone seemed to have these experiences.

Robert bestowed on me a different level of silence, a stillness that was the most purifying. When I saw him, or when I was in his presence, I would be engulfed in the most brilliant white light and be lifted into that space. That is what I remember so vividly about Robert, his ability to take me into that light.

In the beginning, these Satsangs were small, about 50 people, and they were held in different people's homes. Later, one of the devotees and I rented a house with a huge living room and large yard in Sedona and we were able to hold Satsang at one location.

I had the most blessed job as his designated driver. Every day, I would drive him to wherever he needed to be: the doctor's office, to Satsang, or to lunch, back and forth. One of my fondest memories of Robert was whenever I would fill up my gas tank; he wanted to help with the gas cost. It would cost about $50 to fill up my van those days, but Robert, so naïve about day-to-day life, would put a tiny bundle of money into my hand, always $20, to cover the entire gas expense. He was so sweet and childlike and not really interested in gas prices or money. He just wanted to show his love in this most simple way.

Once, I drove him to Los Angeles to see his dentist, who was also Robert's devotee. We stayed at his beach home in Santa Monica, an exquisite three-story building with an unobstructed ocean views. Every bedroom had different colored silk sheets and comforters. There were numerous flower gardens with various fragrant flowers and a variety of plants potted in large artistic containers. Among the luxuries, well-groomed orchids could be found in various rooms and corners throughout the house.

That weeklong trip was great fun! We were treated to nice restaurant meals and we spent 24/7 with Robert. The dentist gave me an expensive Teddy Bear and Robert and I playfully put on a puppet show while we were sitting on the designer couch. It was Robert's grace that put us in a state of bliss more than ever.

Most of the time, the spiritual energy around Robert was intense. We would ask him questions that we thought were important, and Robert would often respond, "What difference does that make?" One afternoon, the energy was thick and electric. We asked a question about something and Robert responded with, "What difference does that make?" We fell into fits of laughter, unable to control ourselves and rolling on the floor. This energy was so alive, and we laughed so much our stomachs hurt.

With reverence to his Being, of course, he never expected to be treated like anything other than a best friend. His devotees were allowed to have fun and play, just like a loving family and he never spoke with authority like teachers do. To me, Robert was a most unusual Guru. He was a pure embodiment of light and grace, a high frequency sage who wore tennis shoes, jogging clothes and a baseball cap wherever he went. If someone tried to touch his feet in adoration, he would stop him or her, since he didn't go for that kind of outward worship. It was his frequency, grace and presence that spoke louder than any "bells and whistles."

Robert did what he could to discourage false devotees. When someone would come to visit Robert for the first time, he often would behave in "silly" ways in order to chase the person away. For example, one gentleman came to visit Robert for the first time and we all went out to lunch. Robert ordered a pasta dish and when the dish arrived, Robert dug in. But instead of eating the pasta, Robert wrapped the strings of spaghetti around his ears, or into his nose and wherever he could on his face, behaving as absurdly as possible.

If people did not get Robert's energetic transmission, they would leave, but for those who could receive his transmission of loving grace, they would be "hooked." I guess this is how the Satsang always stayed at around fifty serious people. I suppose Robert wanted only devoted seekers around him. Of course, this is purely my experience and perception, so others might have seen him differently.

The first Sedona Satsang was held in the living room of my friend's house. Again, some fifty people sat around drooling in the intense energy, enjoying the silence you could almost cut with a knife. Everyone was getting "cooked," as the expression goes. Robert's love was so innocent and so intense, that everyone just cruised along in meditation. Then, quietly, Robert would get up and disappear. After some time, I went to look for him, checking all the rooms after room, until finally, I found him lying on a back room floor, just looking up at the ceiling.

I said, "Robert, you have to come out. Everyone is waiting for you."

He replied, "What for?"

"You are giving Satsang," I replied.

"Tell them to go home," he said.

Suddenly, he grabbed my shawl and made a cape, arms outstretched, much like Superman and started running from side to side of the room, acting as if he was chasing someone. Then, momentarily, I realized that I was that someone. Catching me, he wrapped the shawl around my neck and dragged me around the room. Eventually, I regained some control and pulled him out the door and back to the Satsang room. As he settled into his chair, he looked out over the group and said, "Go home. I have nothing to give to you. Go home now. You already have everything."

He was not interested in playing the role of Guru and perhaps this explains his state of perfection, beyond the Satsang, the teachings or even the Gurus. Robert was just an emanation of extraordinary stillness and pure light.

I learned that Robert was born in New York City in 1928 to a normal family of half Jewish descent. Although his family was not special, Robert most assuredly was. He told me that when he was a baby he used to see a little man come to his crib and speak in a language he didn't understand. Once, when he was older, he went into a bookstore, saw a picture of a familiar man and discovered it was Ramana Maharishi, the same man who came to his cradle when he was a baby. There was an immediate, intense connection between them, but he wouldn't meet his guru, personally, until several years later.

When Robert was a young child and wanted something, he would repeat, "God, God, God," three times and whatever he wanted would manifest. He once told of a time he wanted a violin. "God, God, God," he repeated three times and shortly thereafter, his uncle gave him a violin. He never studied, but would say "God" three times, and the answers would come to him during an exam. I suppose he was born with Siddhis (powers) because once, when he was 14, he took a math test. "God, God, God," he repeated, but this time, instead of the answers, he saw a brilliant light, as bright as a thousand suns. When the math teacher eventually roused him out of his blissful state, the classroom was empty. Incidentally, he flunked that test. After this experience, he was never the same and felt the changes within his inner soul. I assume that was the moment of his enlightenment.

When he was 18, he went to see Paramahansa Yogananda, thinking that Yogananda would perhaps explain why he was so different after that incident in the math class.

Knowing that Robert was already enlightened, Yogananda tried to answer Robert's questions.

"Why do we have to do all these Kriya yoga practices?" Robert asked. "Aren't we already that?"

"You don't have to. You are." Yogananda replied.

Yogananda eventually told Robert, "I know someone like you in India by the name of Ramana Maharishi. You should go see him."

Well, somehow enough money came to Robert and at an early age he packed a few things and went to India. Then I heard that Robert roamed barefoot around India for years, came back to America and then returned to India, wandering around and meditating whenever he could.

Throughout his life, Robert was like a classical wandering Sadhu and people were just spontaneously attracted to him wherever he went, feeling his presence and gathering around him. There would be a group of people who formed a spiritual community around him, but whenever the human dramas of the group started to erupt, like jealousies over finances or Robert's attentions, he would disappear overnight and move on to somewhere else. Then, again, like bees to pollen, Robert's presence became known and another spiritual community would emerge. As soon as the dramas started up again, he would move on. This was how it was explained to me.

When he got Parkinson's disease, he had to settle down instead of roaming around. He chose Los Angeles, and even in the beginning, people would camp outside his apartment gate. Somehow, they must have smelled his spiritual fragrance and came to him like bees to flowers. From this, more organized Satsang groups were formed.

During the time I was with Robert I became an integral part of his day-to-day life, taking him shopping, driving him around town and to keep his doctor and dentist appointments. More than most people, I was blessed with personal experiences that only increased my love and gratitude for Robert, my teacher.

His innocence and lack of interest in mundane matters just highlighted his unconcern for material life. One time, we found ourselves at a shopping mall. As we went about our business, one of the devotees noticed a beautifully embroidered white blouse and said that it would look very nice on me. It was exquisite but also $120, a large sum in those days, especially to a humble non-working devotee like me. Seeing this exchange, Robert pressed a tiny bundle into my hand and whispered, "Go buy the blouse."

When I unrolled the bundle, I found that he had slipped a twenty-dollar bill into my hand. I knew I had to buy the blouse now, even though I was $100 short. The best part of the story was that Robert didn't care about those kinds of matters. To Robert, $20 covered everything; a large tank of gas, an embroidered blouse, a fancy dinner, everything was $20. His innocence of worldly matters was so endearing to me.

Robert didn't care about his popularity as a sage and he wasn't trying to win over devotees. Once, he allowed a video crew to interview him, after their numerous requests had gone unanswered for a long time. Finally, when they were invited in, they spent a great deal of time setting up the cameras, adjusting the microphones and creating just the right lighting effects. At last, Satsang was over and they were allowed to ask their first question. They eagerly began.

"Well, Robert, what is the core of your teachings?"

Robert looked up and said.

"Wake up in the morning. Brush your teeth, have breakfast, and don't let anyone bother you." Then he stood up and asked, "Are you hungry? Let's go eat."

That was the beginning and end of the filmed interview.

Holding Satsang with Robert was similar to Papaji's. First, everyone would go into meditation for thirty minutes. Then, we would get absorbed into the stillness, amplified by Robert. The meditation would be followed with questions and sharing time, followed by Prasad.

I don't remember Robert ever answering any questions. When the devotees asked questions, most of which came from mental activity, they would simply forget what they were trying to ask. The questions would just disappear into nothingness. If Robert ever did answer a question, the answers were always the same.

"All is well." Or, "What difference does that make?"

Sometimes, he would put his thumb up as in "yes" or down as in "no." Sometimes he would tap his head and say, "Hello, is anybody home?" Most likely that meant it was not a good question. In the end, everyone was satisfied; receiving their answers through knowingness, or the questions just vanished. His presence was everything they needed to experience, a "nowhere to go, nothing to do," "no mind" state. It wasn't necessarily the words he spoke or the teachings he expressed, it was his presence and stillness that were enough. He was able to take people to where they needed to be, the very stillness of their minds, where they could witness their minds' chatter, and drop between two thoughts.

Robert took me to a place of inner silence and pure consciousness. There are no words to describe the presence I felt around him. Truly, after years of longing and suffering, God heard me and presented a rare gift. Being in Robert's presence, I experienced God's Presence, as I began to understand "Pure Awareness, Pure Bliss and Pure Consciousness." I began to understand "Big Self versus small self," or "Big I versus small I," all through direct experiences.

One time we were having lunch at a devotee's house and they were firing questions at Robert. Without hesitation, he turned and tapped me on my shoulder.

"You! Answer!" he said.

I remember this moment clearly. All time stopped. I did not even know what the question was. All I could hear was the sound, "Pawh!!" like one hand clapping or the sound of silence. I went into a state where everything was muted and I couldn't hear normal sounds. I felt the boundaries of "Me" and "You," "Us" and "Them," or "Others," just disappear. There was no more duality.

Is this what it means to go into the state of oneness? I didn't feel like I was talking to others or to myself. It was all the same. Everything was me, and I was everything. I certainly had this kind of experience before when I was blissed out, but this time it became real and permanent.

Around Robert I was lifted to another level of Bliss and Consciousness. Spontaneously, his frequency was healing me and wiping out all things that did not belong to my True Self. All my stories, ideas, concepts and dramas were purified effortlessly in his presence. During the last phase of being around Robert, I started to hear celestial music. At first, I thought someone was playing music somewhere, so I would open the door and windows, listening for the source of this sound. I'd ask everyone, "Do you hear that music? Who is playing it?"

They would always answer, "We don't hear anything." I soon discovered that it was the inner music that emanated from within my very own self; it was coming from within me. This inner music, this celestial gift, led me to my next teacher and Master, Thakar Singh.

Thakar Singh:
Light and Sound Initiation

"Know thyself as soul...
We can enjoy as soul because soul is not subject to
change."
-*Thakar Singh*

After Robert passed, I thought I needed to have a secular life; that is, get a job, build relationships and, perhaps, be more functional in the world. I decided to sell my home and all my possessions and travel in my van to Boulder, Colorado. I had no specific plans, per se; I just wanted to follow my heart and my head, and both told me to go to Boulder.

When I arrived in Boulder, I quickly found a local health food store. I had traveled all day, I was hungry and I needed groceries and supplies.

As I entered the store, I immediately noticed a poster on the wall, inviting people to an "inner light and sound meditation initiation program," under the auspices of the Divine Master, Thakar Singh. Although Thakar Singh, himself, was not going to be at this particular program, his "initiators" were going to explain the master's teachings and initiate those ready to begin "Light and Sound Meditation."

In a flash I knew that I was not going to have a normal, secular life. I had no job or responsibilities, so this initiation would be my next step. I was led to Boulder, not to fit into the physical world, but to finally get an explanation for what I had been experiencing all this time.

While I had been sitting with Robert, I would hear specific musical sounds, like a loud, melodic horn, or a powerful conch. At times, I felt like a giant bell was reverberating inside me. The music was always loud and very beautiful and I would find myself looking around to see where this music was coming from. I would ask those nearby if they had heard these sounds, but usually they would reply that they had not.

When I sat with Robert, not only would I be engulfed by these sounds, I would also experience the brilliant light of a thousand suns above me. This sound and light were all inclusive and everything was encompassed by it. I melted into this light and sound and became one with it. It was glorious and wonderful, but I still didn't understand it.

It wasn't until I met my next teacher, Thakar Singh, whose poster I had seen earlier at the Health Food store, that I would learn the significance of these remarkable experiences. Eventually, he would explain the meaning and benefits of this Light and Sound experience, but now, I had no idea what was to come next. Perhaps, once again, I would be taking another, "beyond belief" spiritual journey. With high expectations, I decided to attend the initiation program.

As soon as I made this decision, my inner journey began. I knew it would be an amazing transformation, since I was already having some incredible experiences. However, when I entered the hall on the day of the initiation program, I knew I would never be the same.

From that moment, I was taken into another realm. Even though Thakar Singh was not supposed to be physically present, I saw his physical body walking around the room, initiating people as clearly as anything I had ever seen before. It was so real I couldn't deny it, but considered it was either his energy body or a hallucination. But that, too, I couldn't accept because he seemed so real. Thakar Singh was in the room, manipulating "third eyes" and touching the tops of the initiates' heads. I saw him in this very room, although no one else confirmed seeing this vision. Sometime later, I learned that the

Master promises to always be present at the initiations, so obviously, he was telling the truth.

The initiation program lasted for a couple of hours, during which time; I learned that Thakar Singh was a devotee of Kirpal Singh. He taught the meditation of "Inner Light and Sound" and the lineage of Sant Mat Masters. He was born in 1929, and following the death of his teacher, Kirpal Singh in 1976, he began to teach as a Satguru or Godman.

I listened intently to the presenters, but also I kept my eye on Thakar Singh, walking around the room, keeping his promise. As I watched him, the room became so lit up in a brilliant white light, it was hard for me to see what was happening around me.

The initiators, a man and a woman, presented the "Light and Sound Meditation" and the six rules that must be followed to be successful. Briefly, these rules were: To observe chastity and observe a vegan diet. Don't use narcotics. Don't practice other meditation techniques besides "Light and Sound Meditation." Don't use alcohol or cigarettes, and lastly, don't participate in psychic energy work, Reiki healing, for example.

When it was time for questions and answers, I remained uninvolved in the fiery debate that ensued. People were yelling out questions at the initiators. "Why are these rules important? Why do you think "Light and Sound Meditation" is superior to other forms of meditation? Why can't we participate in psychic energy work? Why can't we practice all of it?"

One man argued, "I have had amazing experiences doing Kundalini yoga, so why can't I practice both?" The initiators responded, "No, Inner Light and Sound Meditation is the highest path." The arguments went back and forth, until eventually, the initiators lost their composure and the male initiator yelled, "If you don't agree, get your own room and lecture about your own path or other yogas!"

I found the situation to be very funny, that the people in the room were arguing about "what was better than what" and the master himself was walking around the room. No one seemed to understand that Thakar Singh was with them all in his ethereal body. But since I was aware of him, I became totally blissed out in his presence.

As I listened, I understood why the "rules" of Light and Sound Meditation were so important, if one were to succeed on this amazing path. First, one cannot be distracted with differing paths, since total concentration and focus is needed. Smiling, I mentally compared this to a husband and wife. If you were married, you would not want your spouse to be involved with various lovers.

In addition, if you follow the path of Light and Sound, you would want to use all your energy, not just part of it, to meditate and achieve liberation. Then, using spiritual energy to heal could lead to the misuse of Shakti energy, so it should only be used for that ultimate purpose of liberation.

I thought that if any of the people in the room knew what they were being given, they would not be arguing about other paths or practices. I had to agree with the initiators and then why were these people here in this room with the Master, if they were happy and content with their current practices? I surely had no desire to let my focus wander, now that I had experienced the Master's presence. So, I completely committed myself, agreed to all the "rules" and gave them the respect they deserved, turning my life over to Thakar Singh.

When the program ended, I was so elated I hurried to a little attic room I had rented in Boulder and sat down to meditate. Immediately, I heard the rustling of clothes. Looking around, I saw Thakar Singh sitting next to me. I remembered that one of the initiators had said, "The Master will be present with every new initiate for six months." He explained that, "He will treat you like a baby in a cradle, giving you the milk of spirituality and will support you in whatever you need to meditate and succeed. He promises to take care of all new initiates, so do not worry." I found that to be true.

On the very same day of the initiation, as I tried this new technique at home, I had the sensation that the Master, himself, was sitting next to me. I turned to him and beaming with love, I recognized him as the very same person who walked around the initiation room earlier in the day. I thought to myself, "How can this be possible?" I knew the answer. It was possible because Thakar Singh had promised and he always kept his word.

I was as "high" as I could be and decided to meditate with this new technique of Light and Sound, day and night. I thought, "Who needs a job or a secular life? This is true living. This is the path to eternal life." All of a sudden, life was wonderful again.

Soon after the initiation in Boulder, I learned that my beloved teacher was going to be in Florida, in his physical form, at a retreat. I couldn't believe my great fortune. He was going to give darshan and I could meet him, in person.

I knew nothing could stop me from going to Florida, so I began making my plans. I gave up my little attic grotto and stayed with another initiate, since she and I were going to travel to Florida together.

We had about a month to prepare for our journey. Since I had already decided that I didn't want to participate in day-to-day activities and life's ensuing dramas, I went into complete silence, communicating by writing as little as possible. My intent was to meditate, meditate and meditate! I wanted to devote my attentions and focus on what was most important to me and the most rewarding, "Light and Sound Meditation." I was consumed and practiced day and night for the entire month, hardly eating or sleeping. I was interested in nothing else, except closing my eyes, listening to the celestial music and seeing the exquisite lights.

I spent my days and nights like this until the retreat in Florida. Then, everything was amplified by the Master's presence at my side. I remember having difficulty walking to the bathroom, as I was so intoxicated with the elixir that was flowing up my spine. The music was so loud and the light was so bright, I could hardly see my surroundings.

Finally the day of meeting Thakar Singh came and I was hardly able to hold myself together. Since I was considered a new initiate, I was escorted to the front of the hall. Immediately, I fell into deep meditation and suddenly I felt the energy in the room shift. Looking up, I saw Thakar Singh walk down the aisle towards his seat at the front of the room. There, in Thakar Singh's full presence, I was immersed in light and sound waves filling the room.

Gazing at my Master, I saw him transform into his beloved teacher, Kirpal Singh, and then into Kirpal's teacher, Sawan Singh. One by one, Thakar Singh transformed into the teachers of his lineage. I sunk to the floor, slowly, like butter melting over the rim of a pot. The lady next to me thought I must have had a stroke or something because she knelt next to me and began shaking me vigorously, whispering loudly, "Are you okay? Are you alive? Talk to me!"

When Satsang ended, I was carried to my room. The entire time I was in Florida at this retreat, I was lost in the exquisite experience of light and sound. If I wasn't hearing a flute playing, then I was hearing a bell chime. Sounds were enveloping me; light was consuming me. The effects of this made me cry all the time, but they weren't the ordinary tears of sadness or even joy. These were the tears of my salvation, the ending of my longing and the fulfillment of all ecstasy.

Sometimes, I tried to muffle my sobs; at other times, I cried recklessly, without control.

In the evenings, Thakar Singh would give a little talk and then lead us all into meditation. While everyone was meditating, the Master would walk around the room touching people's third eyes, giving blessings and basically "cleaning up" peoples' karmic messes. We were supposed to sit obediently with our eyes closed, practicing light and sound meditation. I looked around and saw that everyone was following instructions dutifully.

Being me, I thought, "Now why should I? This is a once in a lifetime opportunity to watch the Master." So, while everyone else meditated, I focused intently on Thakar Singh and the actions he performed. After a while, the Master acknowledged that he felt my gaze, for he would touch someone and then look at me, give a blessing to someone else and then look at me. I couldn't believe I was having so many darshans. When he got to the front row, he stood very close to me and stared directly into my eyes. His gaze was so intense; I felt a tremendous shift in my being as we locked eyes. The gift he bestowed on me, at that moment, opened the entire universe within me. I saw suns, moons, planets and stars, all swirling, like the sky you see on a pitch-black night.

Eventually, the hall monitors sat me by the back door because I was always passing out, or having other intense experiences. Soon I learned this was the best seat in the whole room, since Master was leaving through this door after he put everyone into meditation. Often times, Master would reach the door, then he would turn around, then walk back to me and give me the unforgettable transmission of energy by gazing into my eyes. When I told one of the devotees some of my personal accounts, she exclaimed, "Wow, it must be like when you walk through a field and pass by a beautiful flower. When it catches your attention, you just have to come back and experience it again." And so, when I heard that the Master was next going to Oregon, I made plans to be there, as well.

Driving from Colorado, I arrived at the Lighthouse Farm, a beautiful 300-acre meditation retreat center located in Umpqua, Oregon that Thakar Singh, himself, created. He had several centers throughout the U.S. and referred to them as, "Manav Kendra," meaning, "man-making centers."

As I approached the center, I could feel His Grace's energy radiating light throughout the buildings, lawns and gardens. It was a truly beautiful farm that expressed Thakar Singh's love, blessings, and eminence.

After a few days, one of the Master's assistants came to me and said, "The Master wants to know where you live and what you do."

I told him that I had sold my house, lived in my van and didn't have a job at that time.

"That's great," she replied. "Come with me. The Master wants to see you."

I followed her as she walked me to where the Master stood. Looking straight at me, he said, "You will stay here for six months and meditate."

Then he pointed his finger at the assistant and said, "You will take care of her."

His finger was so powerful, that when he pointed it at me, I began to melt like snow on a sunny day. At the same time, I was filled with incredible energy, fell to the ground and remained immobile, immersed in spiritual bliss.

During the entire time with Thakar Singh in Oregon, I experienced so much love. I had never experienced that much love before and tears of joy spilled without control. The air in the Center was filled with "softness," like a rich liquid form of love and I understood the expression of being in an "ocean of love." I was drowning in my Master's Love and did not want to come up for air.

Being embraced like this, I felt all my ideas, reasons and identities melt away and I was confident that my past karmas were being burned in the furnace of love. Everything the Master had promised was true. He appeared inside my meditations and was with me day and night, whether or not I was asleep, awake or in meditation.

When the Master announced he was leaving for India, my heart was torn between love and sadness. I had to stay behind physically but that did not mean I was separated from my beloved Master. One evening, when my heart was particularly filled with longing for Thakar Singh, I was pulled up to the highest region where the Master appeared in a radiant form of light and I knew that my devotion allowed me to see such a wonderful thing.

As the Master had said, I stayed behind at the Lighthouse Center Oregon for six months and meditated day and night. It is a tradition of the Sant Mat saints to meditate at night, and so that's how I practiced. I learned that some of the Saints would even tie their hair to the ceiling, so they would know if they started to doze off in meditation.

I learned much while I was in Oregon. I learned that Light and Sound meditation is universal and practiced and respected in many religions and on many paths. Many Masters have taught this practice, although not to the extent that my beloved Thakar Singh did. Needless to say, my experience there was life transforming.

Many people are blessed with one teacher. I was blessed with three. Each of these amazing beings taught me everything I needed to know and experience at the time I was with them. They gave me everything, fulfilling so much and showing me the innumerable possibilities in life. I realized that even though I had so many different experiences and paths, one was no better than the others. All the paths led to eternal love and compassion.

Chasing the Sitar

"We are as the flute,
And the music in us is from thee;
* We are as the mountain*
And the echo in us is from thee."
-Rumi

While living in Sedona, my friend encouraged me to learn to play tabla, the Indian drum. It seemed like a reasonable suggestion, so we visited a local musician who played various Indian instruments, including the sitar. This was the first time I ever saw an Indian musical instrument. But when I saw the sitar for the first time, I had an overwhelming feeling of love with waves of heat coming over me. Seeing my reaction to the sitar, the musician asked me if I wanted to hold it. As he extended the instrument toward me and I reached out for it, I suddenly burst into uncontrollable tears along with a deep sense of love.

I could not even touch the sitar, as it was just too overwhelming. The musician said I could come back the next day and try again, knowing it was my first time to view the instrument. I think he appreciated my mystical reaction to it.

With much trepidation, I returned the next day eager to hold this magical instrument. This time I was able to hold the sitar, although I still had an intense emotional reaction. It was more like love at first sight with an extra spray of love potion for the soul.

This mystical encounter prompted me to learn to play this instrument. I called Ali Akbar College and not only registered for the upcoming semester in their sitar class, but also ordered the best sitar they had. I sold everything I owned, including my house, and moved to San Rafael, California where the Ali Akbar College was located. I was definitely consumed with the power of love.

I spent over a year learning the instrument, creating an intimate relationship with the sitar. It was during the initial tuning process that I began to have unique and intriguing experiences. As we all sat in front of the teacher tuning our instruments, I began to spontaneously drift into a meditative state seeing only light and hearing sounds in a sphere other than the instruments in the classroom. At these times, the entire universe seemed to light up as bright as sunshine, and the classroom would be swallowed up in one sound, AUM. The whole universe was vibrating with this primordial sound, generating an ultimate sense of harmony, balance, beauty and pure bliss, all the while beholding this beautiful vision of light. It was almost overwhelming and difficult to describe.

After spending several months enjoying these mystical experiences sitting in the corner of the class room, I decided to take expensive, private classes hoping I would have better luck learning this instrument. But the same thing kept happening to me during every private session. Within a few minutes of tuning my Sitar, everything would transform into light, including my fingers and my body would be so still I would just go into bliss. Most of the time, I felt my body had transformed into ether and I would not even be able to locate my fingers. Needless to say, I did not learn much in private sessions. However, I can say that the experience was definitely a refined state of love and bliss, which words could not describe. Soon I discovered that some teachers felt my state was unique and started to call me "Saraswati," the Goddess of music and knowledge. This was not very good for me, because when the teachers felt this vibration of love it interfered with the teacher student relationship. Finally, I gave up the idea of learning the sitar during this period and I began to surrender to the power of sound vibration to merge into a blissful meditative state. I began to understand why yogis would use

Mantras to undo the various illusions that had been created. I also began to understand how yogis were able to create fire and rain and manifest flowers through playing ragas. I began to understand the power of vibration to the level of subtle thoughts and how these thoughts affect the material realm.

One of my girlfriends, who knew me from Satsang, invited me to an Indian concert in Los Angeles. She said that this group was known to be the best in India and I must not miss this opportunity. She did not know the part of my life, "Chasing the Sitar," nor any of the connections to the sound current experiences. The stage was full with at least twenty musicians with various Indian musical instruments playing ragas in harmony. Again, within a few minutes of hearing the music, I drifted into the brilliant light, going into a place where all sounds merged into one giant AUM. With these professional musicians and their level of perfection in harmony, the most extraordinary vibration was created.

As the concert continued, I became more and more intoxicated, so that when the show ended I had to be carried out like a drunken sailor or overcooked spaghetti. Luckily, my friend understood the effects of meditation and my tendency to go into the Samadhi state. She and I sat in the chair and waited until everyone had left. Then she was able to help me stand up and walk out of the music hall. Whenever I think of that day, I can easily transport myself to that most amazing bliss I had experienced. It felt like an elixir was flowing from the top of my head and through every pore of my body.

After I gave up the idea of learning to play the sitar, I had another opportunity to go to India. A woman who worked at the Ali Akbar College told me that her friend was making a documentary film about the deceased, legendary sitar player, Nikhil Banerji, and he was looking for an assistant to help him with the camera. This was in January 1999, and so I made my second trip to India. Soon after we arrived in Calcutta, I discovered that my health was not strong enough to travel with this producer and be his assistant. God had a different plan for me. I then met a disciple of Nikhil Banerji who was willing to give me sitar lessons. Soon I learned that this teacher was neurotic and had much pain in his body. He was not into teaching anything but was verbally abusive and tried to take advantage of me financially. This was a typical story I later heard about Indian teachers. So, after a few months I moved on after I had made several pilgrimages to certain important sites. During these months, I was able to visit Rama

Krishna's temple in Dakshineswra near Calcutta, then Puri and Orissa which was an eight hour journey from Calcutta.

My visit to Ramakrishna's temple was an extraordinary event, especially since "Ramakrishna and his disciples" made such a powerful impression on me. I really enjoyed the part where Vivekananda meets Ramakrishna. I spent most of the day near the veranda where God so intoxicated Ramakrishna as he met Vivekananda when he was just a young boy. I used to read those pages over and over, sobbing and hoping that one day I, too, would meet my teacher with that kind of magical providence.

When I realized that it was time for me to move on from the illusion of learning to play the sitar, I decided to visit the famous sitar maker, Hiren Roy. Even though I was not successful learning and playing sitar, I wanted to see if I could succeed in owning the best sitar in the world. However, it was interesting that Hiren Roy had passed on and his sons had inherited his skills. They were still making the best sitars in the world. I met Biren Roy, one of Hiren Roy's sons, who was quite drunk at the time, and said "It will take several months to make a sitar for you, but I happen to have a sitar I made for a famous British musician's performance. I don't think he will be coming for serval months to it pick up, so I can sell you his sitar and make him a new one." That sitar had a definite masculine presence, but I purchased that sitar just the same. I regret that I did not ask who the musician was who was supposed to own this sitar. I was so happy about owning this sitar; I paid him and left quickly before he changed his mind. To this day I still have that sitar, and display it in my office as a memory of this love story. I travelled all around India the rest of the year that included the east coast. This six months pilgrimage brought me unforgettable memories for the rest of my time in India. I had to hire extra rickshaws to carry my treasures of sitar and tanpura, as well as my little gas stove and pressure cooker. Of course, there was also my backpack with my whole life's belongings. Sometimes I had three rickshaws carrying all my stuff, one after another. I would be screaming to the drivers not to lose sight of the others. If you have never been to Calcutta and ridden in a rickshaw, you can only imagine the hustle, bustle and chaos of the thousands of people, cars, motorcycles and bicycles, all trying to get somewhere. If God had asked me during that time to give up everything I had, I am not sure I could have done it, since my attachment to the sitar was so strong. It was like looking for the pot of gold at the end of rainbow, or waiting for wings to come out of my shoulder blades so I could fly to the moon with absolute faith. And now, I feel that this incredible time was one of the phases that got me to where I am NOW.

My mystical experience with the sitar amplified my encounter with San Mat path, light and sound meditation by Thakar Singh, which attended to inner music as well as beholding the light of the spiritual eye.

The love I experienced when I saw the sitar for the first time was the Soul that knew the mystery and power of sound. It is said that all these instruments were designed by yogis who heard them first as inner sounds. They created these musical instruments to bring this inner sound to the outer world.

I pursued this love for the sitar for a few years, but finally had to give up learning to play. I just couldn't get past the brilliant light and intense sound of AUM every time I embraced my instrument. Instead, I came to appreciate that the most important lesson was the experience and power of the sound itself, as expressed in this beautiful instrument.

When I got initiated into Sound Current meditation, my sitar experiences made sense and it all came together. Soon I began to hear the sound of silence, the sound of no sound, and within that experience, I heard the sound of celestial music. Today, I hear through the nadis and channels within, as all openings of the body have become their own particular musical instrument.

Having a relationship with Sound Current Meditation, one hears with the inner ear and sees with the inner eye. The sitar is the physical embodiment of this inner sound of AUM and I was able to experience this firsthand as I attempted to learn to play this spiritual instrument of love.

From Monkhood to Marriage

"The meeting of two personalities is like the contact of two chemical substances: if there is any reaction, both are transformed."
-Carl Jung

Returning to America after my second trip to India, I decided to find work since my funds were running low. This was in December 1999, just after Christmas. Once, while in the middle of a job interview, I involuntarily drifted off into a spontaneous meditative state without warning. Needless to say, this was not a quality employers looked for.

Fortunately, I was able to stay at Thakar Singh's east coast retreat center for about six months, often wondering what I was to do next. Previously, I had received a personal letter from Thakar Singh asking me to be a full-time meditator at any of his retreat centers, so I had felt my wish came true. Then suddenly I thought, "I wonder if I could stay in bliss having to pay bills and dealing with the demands of the world?" Or, "Maybe I should find a guy to marry and what about relationship yoga?" With all these thoughts churning in my head, I returned to Cottonwood, Arizona.

After a few days' rest, I went to a yoga class. After class, Gary Nadler, a chiropractor, came to give a little talk about safety in exercise. He was relatively short and was carrying a model spine almost as tall as he was. I thought he had a nice "vibe," and after the class he followed me out to the parking lot and commented on how he liked my questions in class. As I looked at him, in a flash of intuition, I heard an internal knowingness whisper, "This is your husband." This was truly amazing. I came back to Cottonwood and within a week after having the thought of finding a husband, I actually met him in a Safeway, grocery store parking lot.

After a few meetings, Gary handed me fourteen questions he had written some years ago, thinking he would find the perfect relationship or nothing at all. He always imagined the woman he would marry could answer these questions to his satisfaction. The first question was, "What do you see when you look in the mirror?" I replied, "Not much."

By the time Gary got to the fourteenth question, he started wiping tears from his eyes. He said, "You are more than even I asked for."

At the end of that first week, he asked me if I wanted to go steady.

"Go steady? What does that mean," I asked.

"You know, be exclusive to each other only," he responded.

He went on to say something about taking some time to get know each other, and since I did not have the patience or interest in dating per se, I said, "Look at me. If you don't see who I am, don't even bother."

His response? "Well then, we'll just have to get married."

I asked him what made him decide to get married, especially after knowing me such a short time. He confidently replied, "Something tells me that if I miss this opportunity, I will not have another chance to find the perfect person."

What really inspired me to feel okay about accepting his proposal was his promise, "I will never come between you and your God." That was truly music to my heart.

My girlfriend, who is an astrologer, helped us set the date and we were married on Sunday, November 16, 2001 with a simple Japanese tea ceremony. Six guests in our friend's living room were in attendance. Our wedding vow was simply, "Let's set a trap to set us free." For me, this would be the most challenging yoga, the test of

"Relationship Yoga." Somehow I knew that relationship yoga would be the fastest way to set ourselves free.

When I first met Gary, I thought I had arrived at an elevated place spiritually, having achieved inner knowledge and peace. However, I was still impatient, hard-headed, judgmental and resistant to many things in life. During fifteen years of marriage and relationship yoga, I realized I was on a true spiritual path of purification.

I feel that God has given me an amazing man, so I can truly heal the deepest wounds inside me. In retrospect, I now see that my spiritual maturity only occurred through the practice of relationship yoga.

It has been a humbling fifteen years and as I witness my reflection through Gary, I have come to feel safe while learning how to cultivate the unique and special qualities within me. I realized that even though I was expanded in a spiritual sense, I was still scarred and frightened of people and life in this world. Gary was always gentle during this process, so whenever my buttons were pushed, he gave me the space, patiently and with love, to be introspective as I regained my composure. When I see Gary nursing a wounded bird until the bird is able to fly, I am deeply moved by his kindness and tender heart, which was not a familiar experience in my life. For Gary, I am forever and deeply grateful.

Still married fifteen years later, I have come to learn that Gary is my fourth guru, my fourth spiritual teacher. Gary, who does not say a word of spiritual practice, nor claim any path, is a model of what the enlightened person should and could be. He is kind to all beings, all things. He is infinitely patient. He never gets upset, unlike me. He has a great rhythm in his life, at work, during exercise and while enjoying personal time. He is the embodiment of balance and is in harmony with nature and the universe. He loves his work and his patients; he is kind to animals and even insects. And every day he shows his appreciation for all things in his life, including me.

After Thought

"To give service to a single heart by a single act is better than a thousand heads bowing in prayer"
-*Mahatma Gandhi*

In this small book I have made an effort to share some of my stories and colorful life with others who may be interested in similar goals. When I turned 60, I was actually relieved I had made it this far and felt like I had arrived at the end of a confidence course and crossed a finish line. It seems that all the hardships are over, all my questions answered, so that now I can finally enjoy my life until my 'Maker' calls me home.

I wanted to share my story and include the physical and emotional difficulties I encountered as I hung on to invisible strings of light and hope. I overcame darkness and found light. I overcame the complexities of my mind's scrambled misery to find peace, contentment, happiness and bliss. I feel this is a good story to share with others who feel like they are at the end of their rope. If only they can look in the right direction with the right attitude, they will find the answers they seek. If it happened to me, it can happen to anyone. If even a few people become inspired with my story, I will be grateful.

Inside, we all have unconditional love and bliss waiting to be discovered and experienced. If we remove all the complexities that make up the madness of the world, as well as within our minds, we will find that gem inside, waiting to be discovered, the Goddess of Love in all the Madness.

I pray all beings will find peace.

35025822R00085

Made in the USA
San Bernardino, CA
13 June 2016